PEACI

“Here is a book about darkness that [illegible] with light. Jessica Herberger invites her readers into the darkest day in Christian history, Holy Saturday, and welcomes us into the waiting we all still wrestle with in our todays. Drawing from our beloved Adirondack lakes and loons and mountains, she reimagines that dark day of death and helps us to trust that even there, in the unknown, there is still a depth of goodness to be found.”

—**Lore Ferguson Wilbert,** author of *A Curious Faith*, *Handle with Care*, and *The Understory*

“In a world where grief and our lowest places are isolated, ignored, hurried, and even masked with rushing, distraction, avoidance, and excuses, Jess brings us back to the sacred paradox of living simultaneously in peace and pain. Her words brilliantly take the reader through the timeline of Holy Saturday and the personalization for us similarly in the ‘in between spaces’ of our lows and our highs. The spiritual disciplines of lament, rest, and gathering are woven into every chapter, gloriously reflecting the light within us all as believers and the depths to which Jesus lowered himself so we may find victory in and on the other side of our sacred loss. Brilliant. Convicting. Comforting. Amen and Amen.”

—**September McCarthy,** author of *{Why} Motherhood Matters*

“Jessica Herberger manages to take a quiet day that we know little about—Holy Saturday—and offers us a gift we hardly knew we needed. Through careful reading of Scripture and history, compelling narrative, and lived wisdom, she shows us what it means to grieve, feast, endure the quiet, trust what can’t yet be seen, and allow paradox to be an invitation instead of a frustration. *Peace in the Dark* will help you discover fullness within the emptiness of the space between the crucifixion and resurrection, and how—even there in the deepest darkness—Light remains.”

—**Adriel Booker,** author of *Grace Like Scarlett* and *Tethered to Hope*

“Placed between the horror of the cross and joy of the empty tomb, Holy Saturday has much to teach the Christian on life, death, and the persistent challenge of living in the already/not yet. In *Peace in the Dark*, Jessica Herberger explores these paradoxes in a manner that is both profoundly reflective and deeply practical. Illuminating the glories of Holy Saturday with her evocative words and hard-earned wisdom, Jessica speaks gospel truth into the griefs and wounds of life with the deepest compassion and sincerest presence.”

—**Danielle Hitchen,** author of *Sacred Seasons* and the Baby Believer® series

"Grief and silence, loons and the lake. Whatever the state of our heart and wherever we are in the world, we can learn a lot from Holy Saturday. Instead of forced rest, or an unplanned sabbatical, Herberger invites us to see our own stories through the lens of Holy Saturday. This book is a path toward a quiet heart and buoyed spirit in the storm and an invitation to understand our own story and suffering in Christ."

—**Sara Billups,** author of *Orphaned Believers* and the forthcoming *Nervous Systems*

"With the heart of a teacher and a hope formed out of loss, Jessica's words ring true and timeless for all of us who live amidst life's shadows. As a mom who has lost a son, my soul breathed *yes* from beginning to end, and I hope we can all lean in to her invitation to put down our silver linings and dip our toes in the sacred nuance of the in-between, where hollow spaces can be holy places for God to dwell."

—**Sarah E. Westfall,** speaker and author of *The Way of Becoming*

"But what about the in-between? Jessica brings us to Holy Saturday—a day often forgotten between the death and resurrection of Christ. The 'Holy Saturdays' of our lives, all the days between our birth and death, are where God meets us in the mountain highs and valley lows of life. Though the highlight reel of life is shinier and more appealing, we are lovingly encouraged to look at the disappointing, grief-filled days of our lives, uncover them, and allow God's light to shine on them. *Peace in the Dark* gives us permission to not pass over the in-between, dark days but to lovingly embrace them and cover them with a peace that can come only from Christ."

—**Rachael Wade,** Founder of Olive Us, encourager, writer, and Bible teacher

"There's been a shift in me since I read *Peace in the Dark*. Jessica Herberger is a true, warm-hearted teacher and story-teller, and I hope many will take a deeper look with her into this part of Jesus's story. After a season of despair, even as a believer, I didn't realize I needed her invitation to embrace all the ways a Christian life is defined by paradox. I didn't realize I needed to contemplate Holy Saturday, a day I've tended to skip during Holy Week. As it turns out, Holy Saturday is about the reality of my life as it is today, and Herberger writes with such welcome and hope that I'll carry the message of this book with me for a long time. If you're looking for a Christian book to read alone with a journal or with a group of friends, this is it."

—**Amber C. Haines,** author of *The Deep Down Things*, *Wild in the Hollow*, and *The Mother Letters*

PEACE *in the* DARK

FAITHFUL PRACTICES AS WE WAIT FOR THE LIGHT

JESSICA HERBERGER

PEACE IN THE DARK

Faithful Practices as We Wait for the Light

ISBN 978-1-68426-299-1

Printed in the United States of America

Cataloging-in-Publication Data is on file at the Library of Congress, Washington, DC.

Cover design by Greg Jackson, Thinkpen Design
Interior text design by Sandy Armstrong, Strong Design

Leafwood Publishers is an imprint of Abilene Christian University Press
ACU Box 29138
Abilene, Texas 79699

1-877-816-4455
www.leafwoodpublishers.com

24 25 26 27 28 29 30 / 7 6 5 4 3 2 1

For the Originals and our Haven

CONTENTS

ACKNOWLEDGMENTS

Believing in this book has been an act of faith and of casting light into all the dark corners of Scripture as well as my own faith. It has been a true labor of love. For those who descended once again with me, I am forever grateful.

The Originals—For the best life at the lake. For holding my memories and sharing them so generously with my kids. For Claude's brilliant idea of creating our Haven, and for Linda's faithful and fierce stewardship of it, I am indebted. You created my favorite place, and you are a key to the whole thing. And to Mom and Osh for saying yes to the lake and giving us the amazing dream we didn't even know to dream.

The Cairns—You came at just the right time. I don't think anyone encourages quite like we do.

For the friends who remember to ask about the work and earnestly pray for me and for the words as I write: Amy, Renée, Brooke, Mary Ellen, September, Adriel, and Lisa.

Lore—For the gift of your particular friendship and the utter joy it is to be in all of this with you.

Leafwood—For believing in me and this book when it didn't even exist.

My family—For creating Cardiac Hills in tandem, John. For understanding and patience, my kids. For constant companionship, Winston. For sacrifice and partnership and love through all the ascents and descents, Josh.

PREFACE

Having spent much time studying Holy Week over these past years, I knew this day was coming. Saturday. With friends, family, and colleagues, I would share the thoughts and revelations I had about Thursday (the Last Supper and *Break Bread Together*), Friday (Good Friday and *Life Surrendered*), and even Sunday (more to come there). But there was a gap in the middle.

What about the Saturday book?

The question of whether or not to tackle it lingered, and if I did, what would the book be about? After all, the day of Holy Saturday is barely mentioned in the Gospels. It seems an afterthought to even acknowledge it.

How could that be? If it is true, and I believe it is, that every moment of those days matters greatly, what are we to do with the big empty spot called Saturday?

After almost a year in deep study and reflection, I have landed in a new place. Holy Saturday is not a blank space holding up the bookends of Good Friday and Easter Sunday. Nor is it something that can be ignored. For believers, a good majority of our lives are actually spent living in Holy Saturday. The time after Good Friday, but before Easter Sunday, is one of the most overlooked portions of the Bible. Most of us rush ahead to the empty tomb, seeking to find the resurrected Lord. But our lives don't come equipped with a fast-forward button. We all face seasons of waiting and longing for a new or better future. Dead to self, awaiting glory.

Ronald Rolheiser, in his breathtaking masterpiece *Sacred Fire*, says, "As adult Christians today we often find ourselves living in that time between Good Friday and Easter Sunday."[1] That is to say, Holy Saturday is not an afterthought at all. Holy Saturday represents the day-to-day living out of what we believe.

What do we do as we wait for resurrection? Holy Saturday is the answer.

Perhaps you are in Holy Saturday at this very moment. If not now, you have been before and you will again, and it's not the easiest place to be. Holy Saturday is what I call the time when we are waiting on God. Perhaps there has been grief, trauma, disappointment, the death of a dream, and things are not as they are supposed to be. And yet, we must carry on living. The time after a tragedy, a missed opportunity, a bad decision, or a disappointment lands us in Holy Saturday. The times after a death or the death of a dream or the death of a relationship all land us in Holy Saturday.

Our days, here, are spent living in a broken place, recovering from a loss or a hurt, holding on to joy and hope, longing for peace, and navigating the in-between we find ourselves in.

These things—death, disappointment, grief—are the things of life, they are inescapable. A marriage ends, a family member dies, a friend betrays us, a job is lost, a dream remains unrealized. These things happen all throughout our lives. That is why we live,

[1]Ronald Rolheiser, *Sacred Fire: A Vision for a Deeper Human and Christian Maturity* (New York: Penguin Random House, 2017), 99.

for the most part, in the in-between days of Holy Saturday again and again and again.

What, at first glance, seems like an empty day is filled with wisdom beyond our imagination. On Holy Saturday we see space for grieving and lament, for faithfulness and hope. Lessons are passed on through the generations. Best of all, we find peace in the practices of Holy Saturday. The day itself appears empty yet is full. It is a paradox, as all of Holy Saturday is. This makes sense, because following Jesus is, after all, welcoming paradox after paradox into our lives. Up is down; the last are first; there is light in darkness. And it is all there on Saturday.

As it happens, my favorite place on earth is called Paradox. It is a small 896-acre lake in the Adirondack Park of upstate New York, just about five miles long and one mile wide. Paradox is my place of greatest peace, where I lived out the practices of Holy Saturday even when I didn't know what to call them yet. When things have been darkest—and I'll share more of my story in the chapters to come—I have found surpassing comfort there. Paradox has been a steadfast and faithful place for me. Through fifteen years of trial upon trial, this lake stands as my solace and haven.

My family has a camp on Paradox, surrounded by mountains, and it is where I most love to be. The Native Americans that inhabited this land long before I did called it the place where "water runs backward."[2] Typically, a lake has both an outlet and an inlet. The inlet is where water comes into the lake; the outlet is where the water flows out. Most of the time, the outlet is a neighboring stream or river. For our lake, the outlet is the nearby Schroon River,

[2]"About Paradox Lake," Paradox Lake Association, accessed June 8, 2023, https://paradox-lake.com/paradox-lake.

which is connected to another lake, eventually connecting to the Hudson River. Water makes its way south, south, south from the Adirondack Park, through this network of lakes and rivers, and ends up, much like our loons, in the ocean.

On most days, the water from our lake feeds into the Schroon River, following the predictable flow southward, in the most unnoticeable of ways. But sometimes, when there is a great influx of rain or some sudden increase, the water in the Schroon River meets the water at our lake's outlet and overwhelms the usual flow. The water that was heading out of the lake gets pushed back in. The outlet, or exit, becomes an inlet, or entrance, and rather than draining, the lake water swells. This unusual moment—when the water runs backward—is our paradox, and that's how the lake got its name.

The lake is a most precious place to me, one I tend to hold tight to my chest. Only the closest and most special people are invited in to share this space. So you can imagine how surprised I was when, on the last paddle of the season this past fall, I realized that I was going to be sharing this place with you, dear reader. Out in the kayak, a few research books for this project tucked in by my feet, the word paradox was ringing in my head. As I drifted about on the smooth surface of the lake, I realized I was quite literally surrounded by Paradox. At that moment, story after story played in my mind, all taking place at this beloved haven of mine. And I knew I was being asked to share this place in the pages of this book.

So, dear reader, as you face your Holy Saturdays, I offer you a warm welcome and invite you to meet my Paradox. I promise to share her as generously as I can, as God has used her prominently in my life. May you find peace in the dark and a haven of your own as you get to know mine.

PART ONE

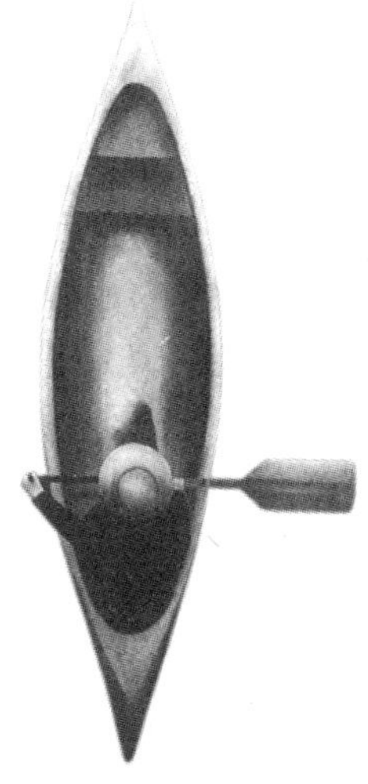

CHAPTER ONE

ACKNOWLEDGE WHERE YOU ARE

"The women who had come with him from Galilee followed along and observed the tomb and how his body was placed." —Luke 23:55

I have a pretty keen sense of direction and can often find my way, even in unfamiliar cities, to my destination. I can draw a map in my mind and chart a course. I can figure out the best parking option and how to get back home again. I tend to not just draw a map in my mind but also know my location on that map. However, this has nothing to do with the type of knowing where you are and acknowledging it that I want to discuss here.

In this case, to know where you are means you understand the specific place in time you inhabit and what circumstances led you there. This is a far more difficult task than knowing the direction to drive your car. To know where you are requires an ability to look around and acknowledge, "This is really happening." When tragedy strikes, this proves to be quite difficult. When we spend time in an ICU or a hospice wing, or even at the lowest point of an argument with one we love, we naturally experience a response of disbelief. "This can't be happening." Acknowledging where you are says, "Yes, yes it is. This is happening." And it is the crucial first step as we sort out what to do, how to respond, and how to live.

It is also the way Holy Saturday begins.

The women who followed along to the tomb were the last people we saw on Good Friday, and they are the first ones we see on Easter Sunday. The women ended Good Friday boldly facing the tomb. Nicodemus had left. Joseph had rolled the stone in place and headed home. But Matthew 27:61 tells us, "Mary Magdalene and the other Mary were seated there, facing the tomb." They faced reality. Jesus had died and was buried. They bravely acknowledged where they were.

Rather than turning away in horror or overwhelm or shame or fear, they stayed. And in staying, they were grounded in a reality that left no room for disbelief. I wonder what it was like for those women as they sat looking at the tomb. I imagine silent tears falling and a hand reached out in comfort as they observed.

Luke 23:55 notes that the women "followed along and observed the tomb and how his body was placed." Observing is something Mary did throughout her life as she found herself in unbelievable realities. To observe is to take notice. She remained present.

On the night of Jesus's birth, all who heard what the shepherds reported were amazed, but Mary's response was to treasure up everything in her heart and meditate (Luke 2:17–19). Mary let it sink in. When they went to the temple for Jesus's circumcision and met Simeon and Anna, Mary heard unbelievable prophecies spoken over her son (Luke 2:25–38), and she was steady. There was no denial, no minimizing.

After a trip to Jerusalem for Passover when Jesus was only twelve, his parents could not find him. When Mary and Joseph made their way back to the temple, we are told that all who heard Jesus teach were "astounded at his understanding" (Luke 2:47). All, that is, but Mary. She was steady. She did not look away. And she "kept all these things in her heart" (Luke 2:51). That is to say, she pondered it all. Even at the edge of his death, she stood steady. John 19:25 says Mary was "standing by the cross." She did not waver, she was present.

And now, at the end of his life, staring at the tomb, Mary's response was the same. She observed and held in her heart all that was happening. Rolheiser says to ponder is "to hold, carry and transform tension so as not to give it back in kind, knowing that whatever energies we do not transform we will transmit."[1] By this definition, Mary does not look away from the mysterious or tragic and, instead, holds it in her heart so that some good may come out of it. This is more than simply accepting reality. Treasuring, pondering, observing, believing. Rolheiser continues, "It is a movement toward the only rays of light, love, and faith that still exist."[2] And it is from that posture that the women stood up and began the next day.

Taking stock of your actual life, whether in a moment of tragedy or mediocrity, takes courage. The world makes it very easy to distract ourselves into disorientation. The barrage of information, the pace of our lives, the fullness of our schedules leaves us running ragged and entirely unaware of where we actually are.

In her book *A Curious Faith*, Lore Ferguson Wilbert traces the questions God asks us and the questions we ask him. The book

---

[1] Ronald Rolheiser, *Sacred Fire: A Vision for a Deeper Human and Christian Maturity* (New York: Penguin Random House, 2017), 147.

[2] Rolheiser, *Sacred Fire*, 149.

begins with the first question asked of people by God . . . Where are you?[3] In the garden, God asked Adam and Eve, in response to their hiding after the fall, "Where are you?" (Gen. 3:9). The question may seem geographical. But the question God was asking pointed to something bigger than just their actual location. What happened? What are you going through? Where are you?

Adam offers a clunky answer. He says he hid out of fear, but that doesn't actually answer the question at hand, does it? God presses in to get to the answers he is actually seeking, the answers that help root us. Questions like "Where are you?" and "How did you get here?" cause self-reflection and require deep honesty. Yet Adam and Eve flounder, offering menial answers to these profound questions.

That is to say, the task of acknowledging where we are is something we have struggled with from the very beginning. Having the ability to know and articulate where we are requires acknowledgment and awareness that slips through our fingers unless we pause to truly absorb what has happened to lead us to our exact moment.

Right now I am in my tiny writing office—so small I can almost touch opposite walls if I stretch my arms wide. Three white walls, one black. I am sitting in a slightly broken office chair in front of a vintage desk we received from Josh's grandmother. This room used to be my daughter's nursery, and before that, it was my mother's dressing room. There is a small window to my right that looks out into the branches of the towering pines in our yard. Around me are stacks and stacks and stacks of books and notes and scraps of paper. In the corner opposite my desk is a favorite rattan chair that I curl up in when I need a break from the desk. It is a precious little space. But all that is simply location.

---

[3] Lore Ferguson Wilbert, "Where Are You? Genesis 3," in *A Curious Faith: The Questions God Asks, We Ask, and We Wish Someone Would Ask Us* (Grand Rapids: Baker, 2022), 28–31.

Where am I? Well, that is a different story. I am exhausted. I am worn out after a month of heaviness in my family's life. Yet also, I am sitting in a faith that has stood, and a marriage that still stands, after a span of more than fifteen years of crisis and stress and trial. I am pretty amazed at that. And as I look around, I realize that I think where I am, today at least, is normal life. And normal life still feels foreign to me. What is so interesting is that if I didn't look up and acknowledge where I am, I would have a hard time noticing that where I currently am is simply normal life. It is hard to identify until we actually look.

The same can be said of those times when we are in crisis. When the unthinkable happens and we need to figure out what to do next, the first step is to acknowledge where we are. My mom is sick; I lost my job; my kids are not thriving; I lost a friendship. Whatever it may be. Acknowledging it is key. That is, facing it. Like the women at the tomb.

Most of the time when we feel lost or have lost our bearings, it is because we haven't looked around and acknowledged where we actually are. This is the paradox of feeling that we are floundering, of not knowing what we are to do. Most often, the floundering dissipates when we pause and allow our souls to catch up with our reality.[4] This is the paradox. We think we are lost when, really, we just haven't taken stock of where we are. We need to begin where we are, and that requires acknowledgment of *where* we are.

So, I ask you, where are you?

Because of the way my losses occurred, and because of my inability to completely acknowledge them in a way that allowed

---

[4] I first found this concept in John Mark Comer's *The Ruthless Elimination of Hurry: How to Stay Emotionally Healthy and Spiritually Alive in the Chaos of the Modern World* (Colorado Springs: WaterBrook, 2020). He cites a story of local porters who insisted on waiting for "their souls to catch up with their bodies" (p. 45).

me to become grounded in the reality of that loss, I found myself floundering in my grief. In rapid-fire style over the course of twenty-four months or so, giving us hardly a moment to catch our breath, never mind get our bearings, I suffered a miscarriage on the verge of the second trimester of my first pregnancy, nursed my mom through a thirteen-month cancer battle followed by her death, and then almost immediately gave birth to our son. All this while caring for my teenage brother facing the same losses, getting him graduated from high school and off to college, providing full-time care for my brain-injured and nonindependent (step) dad, and for good measure, helping my maternal grandmother who needed to get sober and into an assisted living facility. It was busy. And when I say we didn't know where we were most of the time, well, you can see why.

The morning of the one-year anniversary of my mom's passing found me gutted. My son's first birthday was just a day or two away, and I found myself shocked that my mom wasn't going to be there. Shocked. Thoughts kept swirling in my head. Screaming.

I can't believe she is going to miss his first birthday.

I can't believe all she has already missed.

I can't believe this is the story.

I can't believe.

Part of this is the natural course of grief. But even more so, I was floundering because I had not allowed myself the time to take in where I was when she died.

Her illness was a rapid thirteen months of crisis after crisis. Her death was followed very swiftly by the birth of our son, then settling my brother into college, then caring for my dad. The busyness felt like a blessing. I had something to do and someone to serve at all times. But the problem was, all that busyness kept me from looking up and acknowledging fully where I was. I did not allow myself to see, and because of that, the life I was called to live out felt unbelievable.

Subsequently, I was lost. I longed for the light but didn't know how to get there, mainly because I was so shocked by the darkness. I had not been given, nor did I seek out, time to absorb—to ponder—where I was.

For the women of Holy Saturday, their peace was rooted in the steadfastness found, not just in their proximity to Jesus, which they refused to abdicate, but also in their willingness and ability to acknowledge the tragedy that unfolded before their eyes. And this enabled them to face what must come next, with peace. This is how we get through our Holy Saturdays too. We reject busyness and distraction, and we give ourselves the gift of acknowledging where we are.

It took someone finding me the morning of that anniversary, holding my shoulders, looking into my eyes, and truly asking how I was (where I was) to help me name my reality. Finally, I acknowledged how hard and brutal the last two years had been. I named what was going on with me. It was the beginning of my healing. No longer did I feel lost; instead there was, finally, peace. This kind of peace carries on, not despite the grief but alongside it. And it all starts with acknowledging where we are. We must say it out loud.

It's been fourteen years since that May, and still, this practice is needed in my life. Even in these less turbulent times, I find I can be easily disoriented. The best way to root myself in peace is to start by asking myself, "Where are you?" The busyness creeps in, the pace quickens, and we get lost so easily. The way out begins with acknowledging where we are.

As is the case of many northern lakes, every year Paradox is the home to a pair or two of common loons. To call these birds common is itself a paradox. They are fascinating creatures. Here are just a few of the unique qualities of the common loon: both male and female have the same coloration, they mate for very long seasons (five years or longer), they migrate south to the warmer ocean water each winter and then return to their lake again and again, and most fascinating of all is that the partners separate as they migrate south and then reunite each early spring at their lake.

As a loon settles into its familiar water and shore, it begins to seek and wait for its partner. This is where the most haunting of the loon calls, the wail, originates. The wail is a song sung into the darkness that says, "I am here. Where are you?" While nothing can compare to the experience of hearing a loon wail echo across a mountain lake, if you have never heard this hauntingly beautiful sound, it is worth a listen online.[5]

When I am at the lake in the early months of spring, the wail has a weight to it that communicates the hope and longing of the waiting loon. Where are you? Did you make it through winter? How was the ocean? Are you on your way back to me? I am here. Where are you?

The location call, just as it was in the garden, is more than a geographical question. It is a health check. Are you okay? What happened? How did you get here? This is how the loons begin their season at the lake. Settling in to where they are and asking of each other, "Where are you?"

As it happens, I too am grounded by their call out into the dark. I sit on our screen porch, settled into the camp chair that is older than I am, and when I hear the loon call, I exhale.

---

[5] "The Call of the Loon," Loon Preservation Committee, accessed February 16, 2023, https://loon.org/the-call-of-the-loon/.

The sweetest sound is the loon mate's answering wail as they finally find each other. You can hear the calls back and forth to each other as the distance between the two closes.

I am here, where are you?

I am here, where are you?

The loons use this call throughout the season to let their partner know where they are on the lake. One stays with the nest, one goes out to hunt, and all the time, they check in with themselves and with each other using that beautiful wail.

I think this is the call to each of us as we walk out these in-between hours and days and years. A call to be constantly checking in with ourselves and then with those around us, acknowledging where we are and how we got here.

My mom has been gone for fifteen years now. I said to a friend recently, "All my stories lead to dead parents." For a long time, I denied that or resented it. But it is true. And while it may not be the entirety of my story, it *is* my story. It is the reality I bring to all places. Acknowledging it gives me peace. Fighting it leaves me floundering.

Every day, we rise and begin again. And as the loon calls out to another, I say to you, "I am here. Where are you?"

CHAPTER TWO

REMEMBER

"But he told him, 'If they don't listen to Moses and the prophets, they will not be persuaded if someone rises from the dead.'" —Luke 16:31

When I arrive at the lake, the same events occur every time. I back my car into the parking spot, unsure of exactly how close I can get the car to ease unloading while making sure to leave enough space between my tailgate and the front deck. After more than forty years of coming here, twenty-five of them driving my own car, I still don't remember how close to get.

After the car is parked, I scramble out of the car and up the stairs, fling open the screen door, and place my hand on the worn-down brass doorknob of the front door. And then I pause. After just a moment passes, I open the door, and it hits me. The smell of pine. It comes at me like a puff of smoke, like a warm hug, like all my memories wrapped up and running toward me. It is a sacred moment. Every time.

When pressed, I would tell you that is easily my favorite scent. Yet even as I describe it here, the scent eludes me. I think that moment of opening the cabin door and being welcomed by that pleasant aroma is so monumental to me because I forget to remember it until I am there with my hand on that old doorknob.

It can be that way with so many things, can't it? It's not that we forget what is important. We forget to remember.

I find it fascinating the way we have labeled the parts of the Bible. The New Testament. The Old Testament. Goodness, there is so much implied in those names. The present and the past. The relevant and the irrelevant. Yet that is simply not so.

The Old Testament, as we call it, was known in Jesus's time as the law of Moses (or simply the Law) and the Prophets and the Writings. The Law, comprising the first five books of the Bible, and the Prophets were the focus within the temple and synagogue. This is the scripture of the time of Holy Saturday. It was known, studied, pondered, and passed on.

Why does this matter?

Because as we stand at the beginning of a new day, wondering what we are supposed to do and where God is in all of it, we so often forget to remember. We are a forward-looking people. We consider what is to come far more than we consider what has happened. "That's history." We say it as a way to suggest that something is no longer relevant. We are a culture of the now and the future.

It is good to look forward, but to do so in faithfulness, we must look back first.

For the people of Holy Saturday, this was instinctual. They were steeped in the history of who God was and what he said would happen. The Prophets, the Law. They knew it and they remembered. The same cannot so easily be said of us today.

Reading through the Prophets is daunting. And it is far easier to avoid those books than to wrestle with them. Yet Jesus said if a person would not listen to Moses and the prophets, then they would not be persuaded if someone were to rise from the dead (Luke 16:31). In his mind, listening to the books of the Old Testament, in particular the law of Moses and the Prophets, is more impactful than hearing from someone who rose from the dead. This is astounding!

The importance of knowing these books, therefore, cannot be overstated. Understanding God's character is rooted in knowing the history of the prophets. And this is work that must be done by Christians today just as it was done at the time of Jesus. This work cannot be done within the New Testament alone. Brent A. Strawn writes, "'We can't understand the New Testament without the Old' is true as far as it goes, but it doesn't go nearly far enough, since the Old Testament is, all by itself, indispensable for Christian faith."[1]

In knowing Jesus, we know the Father, and to know him, we must spend more time absorbed in the history of those first books of the Bible. This helps us remember God's character in a way that strengthens us.

Remembering God and his promises is the ultimate source of comfort. This is certainly something that Mary and the others relied on in those in-between hours of Holy Saturday, as she had throughout her life. From those early days awaiting Jesus's birth, Mary remembered God, his promises, and his character as a way to make sense of the unbelievable. The Magnificat, the beautiful

[1]Brent A. Strawn, "We Need to Read the Bible Jesus Read," The First Testament (series), *Christianity Today*, January 6, 2020, https://www.christianitytoday.com/ct/2020/january-february/old-first-testament-bible-jesus-read.html.

song of praise Mary offered, is an excellent example of remembering God's character and prophecies as a way of knowing what to do next.

As Mary arrived at Elizabeth's home, pregnant and alone, Elizabeth immediately recognized what was happening and was overwhelmed by it. But Mary remained steady. She knew what and how and why this was happening and gave thanks. This was because she knew the prophecies and that they were being fulfilled.

> He has helped his servant Israel,
> remembering his mercy
> to Abraham and his descendants forever,
> just as he spoke to our ancestors. (Luke 1:54–55)

Mary's response to Elizabeth's amazement was steadiness because she knew God's character and prophecies. She knew the history of what was said and, therefore, knew how to respond in the moment.

How much more could we experience comfort from the prophecies knowing they have been fulfilled in Jesus? We are shown time and time again that God is faithful. This becomes a needed consolation during the uncertain times we all face.

Jesus said, "Don't think that I came to abolish the Law or the Prophets. I did not come to abolish but to fulfill" (Matt. 5:17). Jesus fulfilled not just the Law but also over three hundred Old Testament prophecies.

As we meditate on the history, as we take it in, it becomes ingrained within our understanding of God. As we consider all that was said and all that happened, we assimilate that history into our understanding of the character of God and can then apply that knowledge to our current circumstances. The more time we spend immersed in the Prophets, the more instinctual this becomes to us in the present day. The transfer takes place invisibly, over time, and becomes not just an understanding but an awareness of who God is and how he is that informs our lives.

But there is something else happening here. Mary remembered God, but she also remembered those who walked the hard road before her. Mary, as she proclaimed God in the Magnificat, sounded a lot like Hannah and her triumphant prayer in 1 Samuel. We see the steadiness of Hannah in Mary. Similarly, consider where Mary went: to Elizabeth's house. Elizabeth was acquainted with grief just like Hannah and Mary, and also with triumphant moves of God.

Mary remembered how others had faithfully walked the path before her and was able to use that as a guide for what to do next. We get to do the same thing. This requires vulnerability from ourselves and from those who have gone before us. It requires frankness to be able to say to another, "I know this road, and I can show you the way." When facing the unknown, grief, loss, confusion, whatever it may be, to have someone who has walked before us is a lifeline. Therefore, we must be paying attention. The history that happens around us may very well be the thing we can look back on and remember when we find ourselves facing that next day.

There is another remembering that was likely happening on Holy Saturday as well. It is the remembering of the one who passed. The beauty of remembering is that it gives space to look back at the life lived when there has been a loss. If you have experienced a loss, you know what a joy it is to have another person remember the one you are missing and to be given the permission to do the same yourself. This, too, is looking at history.

When we remember those who passed, or the anniversary of a hard day, or a big milestone, it is a gift to those who are grieving. Until you have walked the long road of grief and loss, it is easy to imagine that calling attention to such things will only cause pain in the remembrance. Yet the opposite is true. The burden is already there. Having someone else remember actually lightens the weight of the dread.

Remembering history brings peace. It brings peace when we remember the movement of God through the ages. It brings peace when we remember those who have walked before us and follow their example. It brings peace when we are given space to hold the memory of the ones we have loved and lost.

History is a powerful thing. It invades a space and soaks into all its surfaces. And if you allow it, it will affect your present. The peace that comes from remembering allows us to be unworried, allows us to be patient, steady. Jesus taught that this is what it means to be in the kingdom of God. In the parable of the wheat and weeds, Jesus tells of a man who sows seed in a field, yet an enemy follows behind and sows weeds. The man's servants are alarmed and ask if they should start pulling the weeds as they sprout. But the man is steady. He demonstrates patience and a sense of being unworried by what appears to be a disaster. "Let both grow together until the harvest. At harvest time I'll tell the reapers: Gather the weeds first and tie them in bundles to burn them, but collect the wheat in my barn" (Matt. 13:30).

This man knows they will both grow, and in time the good plants will have matured, the weeds can be sifted out, and all will be well. Peace. Imagine, we get to experience that, and rather than remember, we rush forward. The more time we spend considering the history, the prophets, the steadiness of God, the more absorbed into our very being it becomes. Our responses become like the sower's, peace filled, unhurried. The history becomes ingrained in us.

All this remembering hinges on one important truth: to remember, we must first know. To remember God, we must know him first. To remember those who walked before us, we must pay attention and observe their walk. This is the work we do to prepare ourselves for our own Holy Saturdays. Spend time with Jesus, read the Prophets and the Psalms, seek community and discipleship with those who have walked the road faithfully. Store up your history so that when it is time to remember, you have a deep well to draw from.

I consider our cabin on the lake to be so precious because of the great deal of history that has happened there. All that life, lived together in the presence of God and his faithfulness, permeates the place. There is a peace that comes from being rooted in such history. It has been God's unexpected gift when I see others experience that very thing as they spend time at the lake. The history transfers. There is a sense not just that it is a special place but that it is a sacred space, that special things have happened there. And with that, they step into the reality such a history creates in the present.

My friend September has experienced this firsthand. When her family was looking for a place to find some respite, I suggested they come to the lake. Since she had never been to the lake, nor (at that point) had we even met each other in person, I was curious what she would experience as she and her family settled in to the cabin. Would it be a nice vacation spot, or could something more transformative happen? With my lived experience with this place, with all the history that has seeped into the walls, could all of that transfer to someone else?

When I asked her if what I thought was happening was really happening, that somehow without a single family member of the cabin present, the history of the place mattered and was impactful, she confirmed it. The history was palpable. Here is how September described it:

> As soon as I set my feet on the pine needles scattering the long winding drive, I felt the untouched sacred peace at the cabin. You cannot erase the effect time has on a place covered in love and preservation of memories. You can't sweep the history off of the porch floorboards or rake the sand on the beach to cover tracks. You can see it in the care, the lived in yet welcoming path through every room and every bookcase, the loons calling your name as if they were waiting for you.

Upon her arrival, September did not know much about the cabin or the deep history it held. Yet the history spoke for itself. It was as if the pine boards themselves held all that needed to be known about the place. And that reality impacted her time at the lake, paving the way for healing and peace and connection that was informed by a history she did not participate in but was still able to understand and apply to her present. The history ingrained in that place, in each pine board, pointed to the peace of God's enduring presence, of the generations that came before and the generations yet to come, all wrapped up in one story of restoration and goodness.

We can become like the boards of pine, the aroma pointing to a rich history we don't have to work to remember (or worry about forgetting to remember), as it is simply absorbed into our understanding of God's character and faithfulness. This is what gives us steadiness in the times of uncertainty. Peace as we face another day.

CHAPTER THREE

BURY WELL

"Listen to us, my lord. You are a prince of God among us. Bury your dead in our finest burial place. None of us will withhold from you his burial place for burying your dead." —Genesis 23:6

Standing on our little beach, you can look to the right and see the beginning point of a bay. This bay holds a tiny little island that I imagine has no actual name, it being of such inconsequential size and in such a remote location. Nevertheless, we call it Dead Boy's Island.[1]

This name was handed to us as children from one of the parents in our community who had spent his own childhood on Paradox. We would pass by the tiny island in a boat and look over to our right and shudder as we all thought the same thing, "dead boy." The legend we told and perpetuated was benign enough, that

[1]There is no official name on any map that I could find but the island itself has recently been named by the family Brend's Island.

a young boy in the 1800s was sick and succumbed to the illness. But what our imaginations filled in was far more captivating. Stories of a boy sick and dying on that island, buried within its shallow earth perhaps. The worst disease any of us had known as children was chicken pox. How could a child die? And what kind of grief would that leave behind for his parents? All these thoughts and tales were wrapped up in the stories we told of the boy the island was named after.

One of the milestones we would reach as kids of Paradox was being a strong enough paddler or rower to make it to Dead Boy's Island without the need for a motorboat. There was a thrill and a dread and a nervousness that would wrap around us as we approached the little island. There was an uneasiness about it. I think what we experienced was an awareness that we were somehow coming, if not face-to-face, then certainly much closer to death than we had ever been before. Death was to be feared, and to come close to Dead Boy's was to come a little too close to the face of death.

It was only as an adult that I had the gumption to get right on the island and sort out what it really was all about. At the time, our oldest was a strong enough kayaker to make it to Dead Boy's. I was up at the lake with the three kids on my own. Not wanting to delay this rite of passage for our oldest, I suggested he could take his younger sister along in his kayak, and I would follow in my own kayak loaded with the remaining sibling.

Off we set.

The kids had heard bits of the legend, but it was the name that drew out the curiosity in them—Dead Boy's Island. As we paddled, they began to pepper me with questions about what had happened to the boy. And I realized I didn't actually know. So as we approached Dead Boy's, I pulled the kayak up and went in search of information. The island was owned by a family who had a small sign hanging on a tree in remembrance of a young boy who had passed away. That was the whole story. There were no gory details, no gruesome lore at all. The story was so much less dramatic than the stories we had kept in our heads as kids.

The whole thing was a bit of a letdown for my own crew. There was no fear or mystery for them. I actually have a picture of the kids in their kayaks as they approached Dead Boy's for the first time. It shows a gorgeous sunny day, blue skies, and above our youngest's head is a camera flare that painted the smallest rainbow. The thing that was so dark to me was a breeze for them.

As we paddled back to our beach that day, I wondered why the different reaction in this younger generation. As I sit here now reflecting on it, I think I finally have the answer. My kids are far more familiar with death than I was at the same ages. They have lost family members that matter deeply to them. They have attended wakes, funerals, burials. They know what it is to love someone who has died. The face of death, the idea of the funeral and burial, is not unfamiliar to them, and in the familiarity, they have lost the fear.

It is easy to assume that because there was a practice of ensuring ritual cleanliness, there was also a distance placed between first-century Jews and the dead. This is not so. The dead required care and almost immediate attention. The body was to be buried the day of passing. This necessitated tending to the body: cleaning it, applying spices and oil, wrapping the body in linen, and placing it in a special chamber or on a shelf within the tomb. The body would remain there for a year to naturally decompose. After a year had passed, the family would return to the tomb to gather the bones and place them in an ossuary, a chest used as the final resting place for the skeletal remains. The ossuary would also remain in the tomb. Burial was an active process, one the family was very involved in and involved in for some time.

One of the great tragedies associated with death by crucifixion was that, traditionally, this meant a lack of a proper burial. This is why it is so monumental that Jesus was buried at all. Joseph of Arimathea boldly stepped out to request and receive the body of Christ to ensure a proper burial for him. As the Sabbath was approaching, that is, Holy Saturday, there was a rush to at least get the body secure in a tomb.

> After he bought some linen cloth, Joseph took him down and wrapped him in the linen. Then he laid him in a tomb cut out of the rock and rolled a stone against the entrance to the tomb. (Mark 15:46)

The Gospels go on to describe how Joseph, Nicodemus, and the women all ensured a proper burial through the application of spices. These hurried moments as the sun was setting and Sabbath was dawning were essential to their next day. Tending to the burial (at least the minimum required, as we know the women returned on Sunday to apply more spices and oils) allowed them all to face the death, tend to the body, and simultaneously tend to their own hearts.

Burying is the work of the living. It is, as Thomas Lynch says, "the longstanding right of the living to declare the dead dead."[2] We must say it and see it and then send them off.

The job of burying well used to stay within the family. The body was cared for by family, displayed in the family home, and then buried in the small family plot. Bit by bit, we have distanced ourselves from all these practices. The widespread adoption of embalming came into practice, then the embalming was no longer

---

[2]Thomas Lynch, *The Depositions: New and Selected Essays on Being and Ceasing to Be* (New York: W. W. Norton, 2021), 18.

done at one's home but at the professional's location, the undertaker or funeral director's home. Then the funeral parlor was born as a way to bring greater comfort and, yes, distance between the living and the dead. What used to be a three-day time of watching and remembering has become an hour or two before the funeral service. What used to be inescapable, the death of the loved one, is now primarily distant from us. Imagine walking from your parlor to the kitchen past the body of your loved one. Today we congregate in public rooms with just enough decor to have it seem comfortable without having it feel like anyone's home in particular and create such massive physical space between us and the dead that we can avoid facing the reality at all costs. The work of burial is no longer ours to bear.

As we continue to distance and outsource such work, we do a disservice to ourselves and our souls. As we distance ourselves from death, we inevitably distance ourselves from our own mortality. And with that, we lose track of our lives. Amanda Held Opelt rightly observes, "The death room no longer exists within the walls of our homes, and mortality no longer occupies our consciousness. The speakable has become unspeakable."[3]

The best way we can resist this is revisiting our attitudes about burial, both the rite of burial (funeral) and the laying to rest of the deceased in the cemetery. Understanding that the funeral is not just a means of saying farewell to the person who died is critical. The funeral is a rite of passage for the living left behind. Planning and attending a funeral is literally how those first days after death are spent. I fear we have lost awareness of how very good this rite is for the living.

For those who can sit in this rite, they will find—I have personally found—a healing. However, as we continue to truncate this rite,

[3] Amanda Held Opelt, *A Hole in the World: Finding Hope in Rituals of Grief and Healing* (New York: Worthy, 2022), 188.

cramming visiting hours directly in front of the service, attempting to wrap the whole thing up with the least amount of inconvenience possible, we rob ourselves of the healing these rites are designed to give. "Funerals," as Thomas Lynch, the only undertaker-poet I have found, so beautifully says, "press the noses of the faithful against the window of their faith."[4] The pressing is good. Yet in our eagerness to avoid death, we miss it, or at best, minimize it.

I think this is another reason we don't like to look too closely at Holy Saturday. It has death all over it. It feels hard and uncomfortable to sit with death in the way Holy Saturday asks of us. How much easier is it to not consider the dead body of Jesus lying in that tomb.

Our eagerness to avoid confronting death has literally transformed how we handle funerals. It has also transformed how we handle burial. In our effort to create distance from death, and the discomfort it brings to us all, we sanitize the entire experience of funerals and burials. I wonder if the distance is simply a guise to bring more comfort to ourselves. Thoughts of caskets, crematoriums, crypts, and the like are considered unpleasant conversation rather than part of what it means to live and die. The burial happens. Might the distance, which we think brings us comfort, only be causing our own souls harm?

As the structure of funerals has been evolving so, too, has our relationship with graveyards and cemeteries. Dr. Russell Moore has written and spoken about the phenomenon of the lost tradition of the church graveyard and its effects on the Christian.[5] I echo his sentiments in that it is important to consider what might happen to a person, internally, as they walk through or next to a graveyard

---

[4] Lynch, *The Depositions*, 52.

[5] Russell Moore, "Should We Miss Our Church Graveyards?" Russell Moore, April 6, 2016, https://www.russellmoore.com/2016/04/06/should-we-miss-our-church-graveyards-2/.

on their way to worship. How might that rightly place oneself in relation to God, humanity, life, and death? How hopeful would it be to experience a tangible reminder of the reunion of the saints and the beautiful truth we live in that death is not the victor as we enter church each Sunday?

Burying well matters because it sustains the living while it honors the dead.

This has been part of the story of God's people from the beginning. When Sarah, Abraham's wife, died, he immediately worked to secure a burial place of honor for her. This is the story told in Genesis 23—Abraham bought land among a foreign people to offer a place of proper burial for his beloved. The act sustained him in his grief and honored her.

Similarly, we see this process active in the burial of Jesus. One of the first honors given to the crucified Christ was for Joseph of Arimathea to secure a proper burial for him. Why? Because it matters. The act was a means for Joseph to honor Jesus and to sustain himself during the grief and shock of what happened. Joseph ensured that a place of honor and remembrance remained. Burying well matters.

My parents are buried in a beautiful, historical rural cemetery called Albany Rural Cemetery (ARC). This is a place where my kids have skipped between the headstones, plucked dandelions and blown away wishes, released prayers into the wind. At first, there was great discussion between Josh and I about appropriate behavior of the kids when at the cemetery. Was it disrespectful to be running about? Do we shush them? Do we expect that they be solely melancholy while in this place? In the end, we decided to let them be. If they can demonstrate joy amid the dead, maybe they are the ones with the right understanding of life and death and God and us. It is they that demonstrate the hope I yearn to cling to.

Our cemetery is very much alive. I find it to be a place unlike most modern cemeteries. Much of that has to do with its history and formation:

> Like most rural cemeteries, following its first burials in 1845, ARC became a very popular destination for family members of the deceased, as well as visitors and tourists from around the world. During this time period public parks did not exist, and rural cemeteries (such as Albany Rural) became the place for people in the city to escape to more natural surroundings for a weekend picnic with the family. Postcards and stereoview pictures of the Cemetery highlight the fact that ARC was a destination for travelers in the late 1800's and early 1900's as well as a tranquil resting place for the deceased.[6]

It is the last sentence of this description that grabs me. A place for the living "as well as a tranquil resting place for the deceased." The peace exists for us all. When I wonder why I like to go to the cemetery and the words of the angel echo in my ear, "Why do you look for the living among the dead?" I start to question if there is really peace to be found among the gravestones. But some days, when I simply grow too weary of the weight of grief, I slip into the car and drive over to Albany Rural. As I pull in to the long winding drive, I see the daffodils and dandelions peeking through the last spring snow, and I remember. It is the comfort and peace, the tranquility, that uniquely inhabits these thin spaces, like the cemetery, that allow me to exhale more easily. It is not that I seek

[6] "ARC History," Albany Rural Cemetery, October 14, 2021, https://albanyruralcemetery.org/arc-history/.

the presence of those who passed, my mom, dad, uncle, all buried among the trees and fields here. It is that I seek the presence of Jesus. And surely he is found in places like this, where death and life meet.

If we can be brave enough, countercultural enough, to not fear death, we can experience profound peace in the midst of it. Welcoming death as a neighbor requires a willingness to welcome discomfort. That is what all this boils down to. We have been trained to consider death a fearful thing. What great peace do we forsake in that? I imagine if we can find a way to set aside the fear and the need for our own comfort, we will find not just peace but Jesus himself.

Paradox is a good fishing lake. This means it has plentiful and desirable fish waiting to be caught on your hook or lure as you cast a line into the fresh, clean waters. Fish like largemouth and smallmouth bass and the great northern pike. While there are all sorts of desirable fish to be captured, there is one that is deemed worthless: "the sunny." The sunny, or sunfish, is actually a bluegill. It is a pretty common fish and, dare I say, easy to catch. There are no bragging rights in bagging a sunny once you are over the age of four. They are the forgotten and forsaken.

Every once in a while, a dead fish gets washed up overnight onto our shore, and it is always a sunny—usually one caught and released haphazardly with damage from a hook or, perhaps, scooped up by a Great Blue Heron and dropped accidentally as the bird flew away. If you head down to the beach the morning after a sunny has washed up, you smell it before you see it. Quick to decay, it does not give off the pleasant odor one hopes to encounter as they bring their mug of coffee to the beach to breathe in that fresh Adirondack air.

I have such an encounter about once a year. Upon discovery, I set out to locate a shovel to scoop said fish up and toss it into the woods, offering a dinner for that evening's crew of raccoons or similar scavengers. Ensuring that, most of all, the smell has been relocated to a much further distance.

This past summer, as I went down to the beach with our youngest, our naturalist, we happened upon a small sunny on the shore. Dead and decaying and, yes, smelly. Finley was upset and concerned. "Don't worry," I said, "it's just a sunny. I will toss it into the woods."

"No!" he responded. "We can't just throw him away. We must bury him."

When I asked Finley why it mattered so much to him, he said, "Mom, because that's what we do when something dies." It is as if my son could not begin the rest of his day until this was dealt with properly. So we dug a hole and buried our sunny. Finley marked the grave with a stick jutting out of the sand so as not to lose track of it. I was impressed with this nine-year-old's willingness to step into the mess of burial rather than toss the dead aside. Thomas Long writes, "In a funeral we are carrying the body of a saint to the place of farewell."[7] And so we did.

"That's better," my son said. And so it was.

---

[7] Thomas G. Long, *Accompany Them with Singing: The Christian Funeral* (Louisville, KY: Westminster John Knox, 2013), 177.

CHAPTER FOUR

REST

"And they rested on the Sabbath according to the commandment." —Luke 23:56

On a perfect fall day last year, two kayakers came along the shore right up to the jetty on our beach. It was a truly glorious day in the Adirondacks, the kind of day that makes you jump in the car and head to the mountains and the lake, ignoring the fact that you have midweek responsibilities. The kind of day that makes you beam with delight as you encounter another person out in the beauty relishing every moment.

Perhaps it was the stunning weather, the colors of the leaves, or the warmth of the sun that day, but joy and a peace radiated off both the men as they smiled and nodded hello. I think they were surprised to encounter another person, as the lake was vacant besides the three of us. Pleasantries passed between us about the lake and the weather and the history of this place that I knew so well. What I noticed most about them was that they were not in a hurry. There was an utter lack of urgency about them and, instead, a presence that pointed to a determination of delight. That is when I found out this day was one of rest for them.

Turns out, these two are pastors, one recently retired, one on sabbatical. It takes courage and vulnerability to even say that in these parts. The fact that I know this detail about them is indicative of a hopefulness that permeated our conversation. We are not just an unchurched area, we are the *most* unchurched area in the country. Eight of the top ten unchurched areas nationwide are within a relatively short drive of this place. That is to say, calling yourself a pastor or someone who follows Jesus comes with a cost and risk. To be a pastor here is to exist in a place of nonstop vocation and ministry. It is hard work, and it is hard work to stop.

Yet as it happened, there we all were on this little lake in the middle of the mountains. Three believers, hanging on. Worshiping and delighting in God and his creation and in no hurry. I think we made each other's day. As they paddled away, I couldn't help but take a pic.

Pastors at rest.

It was beautiful.

If they can do it, so can we.

One of the few things we know for sure about the actual hours of Holy Saturday is that it was the Sabbath. All four Gospels mention this, either by pointing directly to Saturday as the Sabbath or to Friday as the day of preparation, which is the day before the Sabbath, thus indicating Saturday as Sabbath. It is not accidental that Holy Saturday fell on a Sabbath. Therefore, we must consider the ramifications of Sabbath as we live out our actual lives, just as they did on that Sabbath day so many centuries ago.

Sabbath is, in itself, a paradox. In *24/6*, Dr. Matthew Sleeth says, "[After creation] the *piece de resistance* comes out of left field. Up to this point, everything has been created out of nothing, but on the morning of the seventh day, God makes nothing out of something. Rest is brought into being."[1] Created for our good, rest is given as a gift from God.

This practice became one of the distinguishing marks of the Jewish people after Moses commanded the people during the exodus. He instituted a spiritual discipline, dedicating more words to the Sabbath than any of the other Ten Commandments. That practice became one of the distinguishing marks of the people of God, and it continues on, even today.

Jesus taught about the Sabbath throughout his ministry. Early on, he and the disciples were walking through grainfields, hungry, on a Sabbath day. As the disciples plucked some heads of grain to eat, the religious authorities who witnessed this questioned what they were doing, as it was unlawful according to Jewish law. But Jesus responded so brilliantly. In two simple sentences, he affirmed the gift of Sabbath and claimed his lordship over it. "The Sabbath was made for man and not man for the Sabbath. So then, the Son of Man is Lord even of the Sabbath" (Mark 2:27–28). Sabbath is good and ought to be kept, because it is a gift for humanity. It is not a stranglehold. And over all of it, is Jesus.

Sabbath, like any other spiritual discipline, is one that must be lived as a rhythm through all your seasons of life. Just as we continue to pray, we must continue to rest. But how do you rest when, just hours earlier, a loved one died? If we are thinking correctly about rest, about Sabbath, as a spiritual discipline, to ask that question, then, is to ask, "How do you *live your life* when, just hours earlier, a loved one died?" Spiritual practices must be ingrained

---

[1]Matthew Sleeth, *24/6: A Prescription for a Healthier, Happier Life* (Carol Stream, IL: Tyndale, 2012), 23.

into our living so deeply that when we are facing the unexpected, the tragic, the devastating or exhausting, we are not choosing what to do but, rather, simply doing what we have always done. All that to say, to rest in the Lord on Holy Saturday was not a decision, it was simply (and profoundly) their life continuing on.

Sabbath is, first and foremost, a directive. It is the fourth commandment: "Remember the Sabbath day, to keep it holy" (Exod. 20:8). It is something we are called to do. It requires intention. Truth be told, I need to be commanded to rest. I resist it at all turns. I won't exhaust us with all the facts about how busy we all are; we know it because we live it. Busyness is pervasive.

Knowing how hard it is for me to rest on a "normal" day, you can imagine how busy I keep myself during the days of trial and trauma. I am left speechless to think that this day of Holy Week flies in the face of that response. It encourages me, you, all of us, that there is nothing—not a trauma or a trial or a death—that warrants us working, pushing, pressing, all the time. It is good and right to pause and rest.

Practicing rest in the world we find ourselves in today is hard. There is nothing established to help us slow down. In fact, the opposite is true. Our society exists at a pace of 24/7/365. Vacation means working from your cell phone on a beach rather than at your desk at the office. In the social media world, we are actually punished by the all-powerful algorithm when we take breaks. While we have so much data and research to support the need for healthy breaks from social media, the entire system is built around more and more and more. Regardless of your vocation, it is so easy to keep working and that much harder to stop. That is the bad news.

During creation we see a neat and tidy rest. God was done. "For the Lord made the heavens and the earth, the sea, and everything in them in six days; then he rested on the seventh day. Therefore the Lord blessed the Sabbath day and declared it holy," Exodus 20:11

tells us as the fourth commandment is shared for the first time. But we are never done . . . or so we think. This is perhaps why resting is hard for us, but also why we are called to it. To remember we are not God and that he still, in his goodness, desires for us to rest. Sabbath is about surrender. About recognizing our place and finding freedom in it.

In *Garden City*, John Mark Comer shares, "Sabbath isn't just a day to *not* work; it's a day to delight in what one Hebrew poet called 'the work of our hands.' To delight in the life you've carved out in partnership with God, to delight in the world around you, and to delight in God himself."[2] In our family, when we are doing well at practicing the discipline of rest, we ask ourselves a question, similar to what Comer asks his readers: "What will cause me to delight in the Lord and/or is restful to me?" And then we make space for that.

The key here is that this is not mindless rest. This is not scrolling for hours or a television binge. Nor is it about being productive and getting tasks checked off our never-ending to-do list. And it is not uniform or static or prescriptive. The mindset and the intention set the tone. This is the experience of paddling on the lake for me. I connect with God and rest in a way that is palpable.

Go back to that wheat field of Mark 2. Jesus taught about the rethinking of Sabbath that was necessary. He highlighted how the law keepers had twisted rest into rule following more than worship and delight. This is a warning for us today as well. As we began to try on Sabbath as a family, a period of intentional rest and delight and worship, I started making lists of all the things I would not do on that day. All the chores and tasks that bog me down were cast aside. While that may work for some, it did not work for me. The

---

[2] John Mark Comer, *Garden City: Work, Rest, and the Art of Being Human* (Grand Rapids: Zondervan, 2017), 186.

dishes stacked up in the sink, and I dreaded the end of Sabbath as it meant a double workload.

And so, we readjusted. I prepared on the day before, just as they did in the first century, by prepping an easy meal that required less dishes. I let myself delight in the day, and when I felt moved to, I would do the dishes. Not out of obligation or dread. Something else happened, and I found myself enjoying what I would call my most detested chore. The difference was the delight. How I feel as I do dishes on a day of rest is different from how I feel when I do dishes on a random Tuesday. The difference is coming at it from a place of delight.

But even that change took intention. The challenge of rest is in just how much work it takes. But we must not let the need for intentionality or preparation keep us from this most life-giving of practices. "[The Sabbath] is not an interlude but the climax of living."[3] Living a life of disciplined rest is a beautiful way to live differently than the world. To remind ourselves and those in our orbits that Sabbath is a gift, rest is for our good, and none of us are so important that the world hinges on our keeping going points to the kingdom of God in a way that is so compelling.

Specific to our study of Holy Saturday, it is fascinating to consider Sabbath as not just the best of life but also as pointing to eternal life. Rabbi Abraham Heschel, in his powerful book *The Sabbath*, shares that, "According to the Talmud, the Sabbath is *olam* ha-ba, which means: somewhat like eternity or the world to come."[4] The Rabbi continues, "The world to come is therefore not only a posthumous condition, dawning upon the soul on the morrow after its departure from the body. The essence of the world to come is Sabbath eternal, and the seventh day in time is an example

---

[3] Abraham Joshua Heschel, *The Sabbath: Its Meaning for Modern Man* (New York: Farrar, Straus and Giroux, 2005), 14.

[4] Heschel, *The Sabbath*, 74.

of eternity."[5] Eternity awaits. A place of unceasing worship and delight. This is what Sabbath points us to.

Again, I am awestruck at the timing of Holy Week and how this invitation to rest and taste the beauty of eternity is so perfectly aligned with the death of Jesus and how we are to live as we wait for resurrection. The gift of rest, the gift of Sabbath, points us to the fact that even here on earth as we wait, we may taste the goodness of what is to come. To rest, to worship, to delight. And to do so amid any circumstances.

"Come to me, all of you who are weary and burdened, and I will give you rest," Jesus tells us (Matt. 11:28). To get to taste eternity as we are burdened is a joy. Resting allows us a taste of eternity and points us to the reality of heaven, all while in the middle of our everyday lives.

None of this works, however, if we don't remember. We must remember to hold this practice close. After Moses received the Ten Commandments in Exodus chapter 20, the whole thing fell apart fairly quickly. The people of God had forgotten. They created idols. They forgot God and their place as his people. They forgot that God had saved them! When God and Moses try this again; they re-present the Ten Commandments. Notice what is written about Sabbath. "Be careful to remember the Sabbath day, to keep it holy as the Lord your God has commanded you" (Deut. 5:12). Be careful, God warns. But then he goes on. Verse 15 is so important to our understanding of Sabbath: "Remember that you were a slave in the land of Egypt, and the Lord your God brought you out of there with a strong hand and an outstretched arm. That is why the Lord your God has commanded you to keep the Sabbath day."

The toiling, the unending work, the pace of producing more and more and more. That was Egypt. And goodness, if that isn't

---

[5] Heschel, *The Sabbath*, 74.

our world today too. But God tells us to be careful and remember that is not who we are. Hear me, it is not who we are.

Sabbath reminds us we are not slaves. But we must be careful to remember.

Sabbath is the time of shalom, the state of wholeness and peace. Shalom speaks to well-being and restoration. Heschel says the Sabbath is a "day of harmony and peace, peace between man and man, peace within man, and peace with all things."[6] When we rest, we declare that all is well. Sometimes the words are a declaration. Sometimes the words are a prayer. All is well; all will be well. We forget this truth, and so God weaves into the fabric of each week a time for us to remember the shalom we have.

The rhythms of rest, of Sabbath, serve us all the time. Yet when we are in times of trial or turmoil, those rhythms serve us in particularly profound ways. A few years ago, I began making a simple coffee cake on Saturday morning. A few weeks in a row of this rhythm and it had stuck. The coffee cake marked our Saturday morning. As I set the cast iron pan down on the table, it signaled that Saturday morning was different from the grind of the weekdays. The coffee cake rhythm of our restful Saturday mornings served my family in immeasurable ways when we found ourselves in a time of trials and urgent caretaking and advocating. The days began to bleed together. We were just getting through in a haze. But then, when Saturday came around and the coffee cake sat on the table, we all let out a collective exhale. Rest. All is well. Shalom.

The shalom we experience during rest, during Sabbath, offers a pause in the face of uncertainty. Shalom declares there is wholeness. When extended as a greeting, it becomes a prayer. All is well; all will be well. No matter how busy we are, why would we forsake

---

[6] Heschel, *The Sabbath*, 31.

such a blessing? To rest is to join the generations praying words of peace upon the people of God.

Imagine the beauty of Sabbath being the day after Jesus died on the cross. A day to rest in the finished work of Christ and all the things accomplished on the cross just hours before. This is Sabbath at its core. When they greeted each other, "Shabbat shalom," that night, never had the words been truer. Even though they had not yet experienced the resurrection of Easter, those first-century followers were prompted, commanded, to rest. And so they did.

The edge of our beach is lined with rocks, a jetty. The line of rocks juts out into the water forming a beautiful landscape, home to minnows and crayfish and snails. In a lake, a jetty primarily exists, however, to hold the sand in place. Our little beach has had a jetty since the 1950s or earlier. For a while, we had one of only a few jetties on the lake, and as such, we inherited all the light sand that would wash down the shore. The jetty commands the sand to stop and stay.

As I walk on our beach and feel that light sand in between my toes, I feel, like the sand, I need to be caused to stop. When I flop in my beach chair, book at my side, and let out that big exhale, I feel like the grains of sand crashing into the rocks as my forward motion is abruptly halted. Just like the grains of sand, eventually I settle in and begin to experience a true rest. On days like this, I mark my rest by stacking a rock tower, a cairn, on the jetty.

Cairns are used as trail markers in the forests of parks and along hikes. "Yes," the rocks call out, "this is the way to go." But cairns are also memorials. They are a means of remembering. We see this throughout the Bible as piles of rocks are erected. The rocks then stand as witnesses to what happened. I think my cairns do both.

As I crouch in the water at the farthest point of the jetty, rock in hand, I begin my stack. I take my time as I look for just the right rocks to fit together. Lake rocks are not the smooth ovals you see on the shores of the ocean. No, lake rocks are craggy, odd shapes covered in moss. By the time I am done, it is just a handful of stones precariously held together by tension, defying gravity. This is what Sabbath feels like to me.

Sitting on the beach or looking down from the porch, I watch my cairn all day. Yes, I think, a memorial to rest. A way to remember that I rested and it was good. The cairns never last too long. The far point of the jetty offers minimal shelter from the waves or the wake of a boat. By the next morning, the cairn has usually toppled into the water, awaiting the next Sabbath, when I will settle in to the beach like a grain of sand and then, ever so slowly, make my way to the jetty again and begin stacking.

PART TWO

CHAPTER FIVE

THE BEAUTY OF LAMENT

"In my distress I called to the LORD." —Psalm 120:1

Our lake is not just situated within the Adirondack Mountains, it is quite literally surrounded by them. As such, the echo that reverberates across the water is really something. You can hear the sound bouncing about between the mountains and over the water as it continues on. When they were younger, our kids would stand on the edge of the water and yell, "Echo!" They listened to their words ricochet from mountaintop to mountaintop and back to them, amazed at the power of their voices as they heard their cries reverberating all around. "Echo! Echo. Echo . . ."

The wilderness does the same thing. There is a loon call known as the tremolo. The tremolo is used to call out in times of distress. When humans are too close, when boats are speeding by, when predators are lurking, the loon cries out using the tremolo. While the wail call of the loon has an eeriness to it, the tremolo is more musical. It sounds like a yodel or a series of trills. The sound comes from deep in the throat, neck stretched out, head sometimes shaking back and forth.

The tremolo is often used by the pair of loons. They surround the danger and amplify their cries. Where there was one voice, now there are two. On our lake, surrounded by mountains, the tremolos of a pair of loons echo against the earth, against the trees. Where there are two loons, it can sound like a multitude. The sound waves of the tremolos crash directly into each other, splintering and falling on every surface, crying out with abandon for all to hear that all is not well.

In *Walden*, Thoreau describes the tremolo of his loon similarly, "This was his looning, perhaps the wildest sound that is ever heard here, making the woods ring far and wide."[1] The wildest sound ever heard. Reacting to the common loon's tremolo call, writer John McPhee reflected, "If he were human it would be the laugh of the deeply insane."[2]

But perhaps it isn't insanity, it's just that we don't know the language of lament.

Lament is a cry out to the Creator of the universe that all is not well. It is both a plea for help and praise to God. Lament is a cry for deliverance. Lament is vocalizing frustration and disappointment. Lament declares when things are amiss, that right and wrong are upside down. It asks the hard questions and says the things out loud that we tend to hold inside.

"Why?"

"How long?"

---

[1] Henry David Thoreau, *Walden; or, Life in the Woods and Civil Disobedience* (1849; reprint, New York: Random House, 2014), 188.

[2] Tom Klein, *Loon Magic* (Minocqua, WI: NorthWord Press, 1996), 68.

"How can this be so?"

But lament also acknowledges God's desires for our good and our flourishing. In lament, we celebrate and acknowledge that he can handle these hard questions as we cry out from the deepest parts of ourselves. Lament honors God and our relationship with him. Lament is healing. Lament is so multidimensional that I fear we have lost understanding of it.

In *Prophetic Lament*, Soong-Chan Rah notes that we do not even have the habit or opportunity to sing lament within our congregations: "Christian Copyright Licensing International (CCLI) licenses local churches in the use of contemporary worship songs and tracks the songs that are most frequently sung in local churches. CCLI's list of the top one hundred worship songs in August of 2012 reveals that only five of the songs would qualify as a lament."[3] The beauty, the comfort, of crying out to God as a people has been lost. The consolation and connection singing in lament can bring has been in a rapid decline. This comfort and connection so beautifully found in the African American spirituals has been swept away. It is tragic.

Lament simply does not fit our modern sensibilities. In our world of packaged Christianity, of shiny social media and messages that get wrapped up in a bow with a happy ending or a lesson learned, or a rapid-fire hot take of outrage, how do we understand the language of lament?

Lament is a way to acknowledge the wrongs of this world and offer dignity to suffering. Lament is also a way to connect with God; it is relational. But in order for us to show up in this relationship, we must be honest. To lament is to voice not just anger but the hurt, the betrayal, the disappointment, the outrage. Are

---

[3] Soong-Chan Rah, *Prophetic Lament: A Call for Justice in Troubled Times* (Downers Grove, IL: InterVarsity Press, 2015), 22.

we vulnerable enough with God to show that? And then to do so while still praising? This is what we are called to do.

I wonder how welcoming we are to this concept. We get angry. We raise our voices. We even condemn God. But do we, could we, approach him, recognizing our trust in him, calling out the hurt we are feeling and begging for a change, with praise on our lips?

Lament is good. It is "a true and honest expression of our pain to God . . . [that] is not only good, it is holy—a sign of a covenant partnership and trust in a holy God. Lament is an appropriate response to evil in the world."[4] I imagine our ability to respond in such a way to the world of outrage we find ourselves in would be so countercultural and revolutionary that all would take notice. This is a unique opportunity we have. But without stepping into lament, we miss it.

It is a language we need to relearn.

The first-century followers of Jesus fluently spoke the language of lament. Not only is the entire book of Lamentations a lament but the book of Psalms also contains many, many expressions of lament. More than half of Psalms is made of psalms of lament.

One impactful psalm of lament is the first of the Songs of Ascent, the collection of fifteen Psalms (Pss. 120–34) that were traditionally sung as pilgrims climbed the long uphill road to Jerusalem that ultimately led to the temple. Pilgrims made this journey three times a year for the Festival of Passover (Pesach), Festival of Weeks/Pentecost (Shavuot), and Festival of Booths/Shelters (Sukkot) as commanded in Deuteronomy 16:16. Psalm 120, a psalm of lament, is how the Jewish pilgrims began their journey. As they sang these songs, they would draw closer to Jerusalem while, quite literally, ascending. As their bodies and eyes were lifted up to the temple and to God, they were simultaneously climbing

[4] "Lamentations," Old Testament Overviews, BibleProject, accessed February 26, 2023, https://bibleproject.com/explore/video/lamentations/.

a steep road and singing these songs that kept them going along that journey.

These are the same songs that Joseph, Mary, and young Jesus would likely have sung as they made their pilgrimage to Jerusalem (Luke 2:42–51). And they were the same songs pilgrims would have been singing just days before, or even the day of Good Friday, the day Jesus was crucified, as they arrived for Passover. The words of Psalm 120:1–2 would have been fresh in their minds the next day.

> In my distress I called to the Lord,
> and he answered me.
> "Lord, rescue me from lying lips
> and a deceitful tongue."

In just these first two verses, we can see the cry for help, the acknowledgment that all is not well, and the relationship with God. These are the marks of lament. I like how theologian Glenn Packiam outlines lament as a form of praise, proof of relationship, pathway to intimacy with God, prayer for God to act, and participation in the pain of others.[5]

Psalm 120 in its entirety is pretty rough. When I read through it, I get bristly. It feels too raw, too gripey, too much complaining. "Isn't there a bright side?" I want to ask the pilgrims. Doesn't speaking like that of God, to God, cause you to feel distant from him? And to imagine, this is how they start their celebration as they embark to Jerusalem for the festivals? But yes, this is how the journey to the feasts and festivals began. This is how the journey to the temple, the place that represented the dwelling place of God, began. Because lament is relational. In honesty and humility, as

[5] Glenn Packiam, "Five Things to Know about Lament," N. T. Wright Online, April 3, 2020, https://www.ntwrightonline.org/five-things-to-know-about-lament/.

their feet brought them, step by step, closer to God, they lamented, and it too brought them, word by word, closer to God.

This is the true paradox of lament. Where we may see ourselves sinking low or see a distance forming between ourselves and God as we press into lament, the pilgrims show us that the opposite is true. They lamented and drew closer to God. With each step, they were brought closer into the presence of the Lord and the temple. We think allowing the lament to overtake us will send us into a pit when that could not be further from the truth. But the truth is, the lament brings the ascent. As we cry out to God, we, like the pilgrims, rise.

Welcoming lament also looks like welcoming the lament of others. As Packiam notes, it is "participation in the pain of others."[6] Lament offers no platitudes. Lament acknowledges that there is pain, injustice, sin. Lament approaches with hope and reverence for God, but it is not a neat and tidy hope, wrapped up with a bow and a plucked Scripture verse. Lament is weeping, mourning, grieving on behalf of others just as much as it is on behalf of ourselves. Many of the psalms of lament are communal in nature. They are cries to God for others.

What can we do when we see the pain of those we cherish? We must cry out with them and for them. By meeting them right where they are, we offer a glimpse of connection, to us, yes, but more importantly, to God. It is a way for us to be people of the kingdom come. Beloved theologian and professor N. T. Wright says, "When the world is going through great convulsions, the followers of Jesus are called to be people of prayer in the place where the world is in pain."[7] This is lamenting.

---

[6] Packiam, "Five Things to Know about Lament."

[7] N. T. Wright, *God and the Pandemic: A Christian Reflection on the Coronavirus and Its Aftermath* (Grand Rapids: Zondervan Reflective, 2020), 42.

Most beautiful of all, when we lament, we experience an intimacy with God. Lament is something Jesus did. That verse we know so well, the shortest verse in the Bible, "Jesus wept" (John 11:35), is about lament. The word "wept" is *drkryo*; it is a synonym to *threneo*, that is, lament. Jesus lamented. And so as we lament, we join him. In the same breath that we call out to God, we also join in with God. It's a miraculous thing.

On the cross, Christ called out, "My God, my God, why have you forsaken me?" These words, taken from Psalm 22, aren't some sort of memory verse for Jesus. He isn't thinking about David, who might have been the author. Faced with the agony and isolation of the cross, Jesus took these words of lament and made them his own.

While it might be a little offensive to our modern ears to hear the word "forsaken" spoken of God, Jesus cried out on instinct. He poured over Psalms day-by-day as many of the Jews of his time did. And they gave true voice to his suffering. The psalm continues on to declare God's faithfulness and goodness. Look at verses 24 and 25:

> He did not hide his face from him
> but listened when he cried to him for help.
> I will give praise in the great assembly
> because of you;
> I will fulfill my vows
> before those who fear you.

God listened when the psalmist cried to him for help. Lament is welcome, expected even. And when we hold back, we create distance between ourselves and God. Lament is what closes the gap.

God is there in all of it. It is our call to join him.

In an immediate sense for us today, as we lament, we join in with Jesus interceding on our behalf. When I lament, I also yearn to be able to cry out, "I will give praise." But often, I am not able to do so. In the moments when the praise feels out of reach, there is a tremendous gift in realizing that Jesus praises for us just as he laments.

There was lament that Saturday. And with it, comfort and connection were found. This is what we get to experience in our lives as we press into the language of lament. The cries of anguish can be intimidating when they come out of our throats or those of the ones we love. Perhaps the greatest comfort we can experience at times like this is when we realize that Jesus is crying out with us and for us as well. Jesus, who intercedes on our behalf, joins us in our cries.

Lament is guttural. The sounds of lament can seem, to our untrained ears, harsh, aggressive, even offensive. Yet as we recognize the goodness that comes in that raw vulnerability, the call to a God who hears and a God who cries out with us, the anguish becomes beautiful.

At the lake, when we hear a loon cry out, regardless of what is going on, we make our way to the screened porch to listen. The sound is one I have never tired of, and I don't think I ever will. It is captivating.

Last fall, Josh and I were in the living room, fire crackling in the wood stove to stave off the chill air. We were sunk deep into the comfy furniture, watching the flames and reading, when we heard it. The tremolo. Like moths to a flame, we were drawn out to the porch to listen. First there was one loon, then another, then the echoes began. That season we had two loon pairs on the lake, and before we knew it, the second pair had joined in, and we could hear them from the other side of the narrows. There was trouble. All was not well, and the loons were crying out. We looked at each other with awe and concern. Concern, because clearly something was amiss. The noise was louder than we had ever heard. It was desperate. But also, awe, because the sound of those loons, joining together, echoing across the mountains as creation itself cried out with them, was breathtaking.

"Oh Lord, something isn't right. Protect them," I prayed, as I, too, joined the chorus of the crying out.

Oliver Austin said, "No one who has ever heard the uninhibited, cacophonous, crazy laughter can ever forget it."[8] Austin is right in that it is unforgettable. But I take issue with Austin or McPhee calling it the sound of insanity or "crazy laughter." The tremolo isn't crazy.

It is lament. And it is a beautiful sound.

---

[8] Klein, *Loon Magic*, 66.

CHAPTER SIX

STAND IN THE GAP

"I searched for a man among them who would repair the wall and stand in the gap before me." —Ezekiel 22:30

Living on the water's edge, we have lots of rescue missions for lost items. As the water laps at the shore, we watch sand shovels or tossed-aside tubes begin to float and then drift further into the lake. "Go grab the tube!" I proclaim as I watch it get pulled away. Usually it requires just a step or two into the water before the item is reclaimed and placed back on solid ground.

Sometimes the rescue missions are a bit more dramatic. I have woken up to missing kayaks, the misty morning having claimed the boats for itself as I see their yellow and orange colors drifting aimlessly in the middle of the lake.

Most dramatic of all is when our inflatable trampoline that is weighted down to the bottom of the lake takes off. A large circle, about eight feet in diameter, it has several cinder blocks dropped into the water to hold it in place. But when a good wind comes through, the inflatable stands no chance of staying put. It pushes down the lake, like a sail, and as it goes, the cinder blocks become heavier, collecting more of the muck and mire of the deep. So when it has finally settled in its new location, two things are immediately clear: it is not where it is supposed to be, and it is held captive by the weight of the muck of the deep.

A few years ago, this exact situation occurred, and the following day, friends from home arrived to the cabin. They stood on the beach and pointed off to the right to the inflatable, obviously in a spot where no one would use it or swim to it. "What's it doing over there?!" they asked. After we described to them the woe of the wind dragging it away and how it felt hopeless to even have this displaced thing, they replied, "Well, let's go get it."

Simple as that, a rescue mission had begun.

Our friend, his son, and Josh all climbed into the rowboat to go check out the state of the inflatable and reclaim it. They jumped in the rowboat, one in charge of the oars, one leaning over the edge looking into the water, and one at the bow of the boat, eyes straight ahead, coaxing them all on. If you are picturing George Washington crossing the Potomac, then you have a pretty accurate visual of what was happening.

Upon approaching, they wrestled and wrestled with the ropes to attempt to free it and drag it back to its rightful location. After a long attempt using all the force they had to get the cinder blocks out of the muck, they realized it was futile. The only way to get it back was to cut it free.

I will never forget the image of them slowly rowing back, hanging on to the short ends of the ropes for dear life, determined to save what was most important. That's what rescue missions are all about.

This is where things get tricky. We know that Jesus, the man, died on Good Friday and was buried in Joseph's tomb. There was a true death as he was fully man. But the other part . . .

Here are Jesus's own words describing what lay ahead for him: "For as Jonah was in the belly of the huge fish three days and three nights, so the Son of Man will be in the heart of the earth three days and three nights" (Matt. 12:40).

In other words, what *else* was happening on Holy Saturday while the body of Jesus lay in the tomb?

That singular question, *what else?*, could easily have overtaken this whole book, just as it traditionally takes over any discussion regarding Holy Saturday. This was the piece of the puzzle that held me up in a year of research and wrestling. I want to take you on a quick tour of where the main schools of theology land. A basic starting point is the Apostle's Creed, that quintessential summary of the beliefs of the church, which begins:

> I believe in God,
> the Father almighty,
> Creator of heaven and earth,
> and in Jesus Christ, his only Son, our Lord,
> who was conceived by the Holy Spirit,
> born of the Virgin Mary,
> suffered under Pontius Pilate,
> was crucified, died and was buried;
> he descended into hell;
> on the third day he rose again from the dead.

What does that mean, "he descended into hell"? Where exactly did Jesus go? Was it him or his spirit? Was it a victorious trip or one of condemnation? These are just some of the questions that you could ask from this one statement of belief.

Scripturally, we have a few essential passages to consider. Let's start with Peter's words. In his sermon at Pentecost (Acts 2:27), Peter quotes Psalm 16:9–10 (NIV):

> My heart is glad and my tongue rejoices;
> my body also will rest secure,
> because you will not abandon me to the realm of
> the dead,
> nor will you let your faithful one see decay.

He notes that the patriarch David had died and was buried, but his psalm "spoke of the resurrection of the Messiah, that he was not abandoned to the realm of the dead, nor did his body see decay" (Acts 2:31 NIV). Then later in his letters, Peter makes two more statements about Christ's death and his preaching among the spirits and among those "now dead."

> For Christ also suffered for sins once for all, the righteous for the unrighteous, that he might bring you to God. He was put to death in the flesh but made alive by the Spirit, in which he also went and made proclamation to the spirits in prison who in the past were disobedient. (1 Pet. 3:18–20)

> For this reason the gospel was also preached to those who are now dead, so that, although they might be judged in the flesh according to human standards, they might live in the spirit according to God's standards. (1 Pet. 4:6)

And we have the words of Jesus from the book of Revelation, "I was dead, but look—I am alive forever and ever, and I hold the keys of death and Hades" (Rev. 1:18).

When we examine these scriptures and the Apostle's Creed, we need to remember that hell, as used in the creed, is not the place of eternal damnation. The creed, and the scriptures, are referring to the place of the righteous dead. This is *Sheol* (Hebrew) or *Hades* (Greek). Scripture has also called it paradise or Abraham's bosom (Luke 16:22). All these are words to describe the place of death where all of humanity would wait for the redemption of the Messiah.

The concept of the underworld, Sheol or Hades, was far more prevalent in the culture of the first century. What seems mythological and foreign to us was simply taken for granted. I wonder if this points back to the distance we have drawn out between ourselves and death? Perhaps our gradual pulling away from any personal connection with physical death has allowed space for greater confusion to settle in during our current time.

"What did he do?" is the question that causes the most division.

John Calvin, Karl Barth, and most adherents of the Reformed tradition explain that the creedal declaration "descended into hell" is figurative. That Christ, condemned, suffered all the horrors of hell on the cross on Good Friday. The descent is the moment on the cross when Christ bears the burden of sin. This leaves Christ's body in the tomb on Saturday; there was no actual descent to the place of the dead.

Next we have twentieth-century Catholic theologian Hans Urs von Balthasar's suggestion that Christ did literally descend to hell (Sheol/Hades), but he did so in a state of condemnation. In hell, Balthasar claims, Jesus, as God, experienced the punishment in full, thus creating a second death. The third volume of his provocative Theo-drama that explores this theory, written in 1978, continues to be debated by theologians.

A third approach has Christ, fully God, descending to hell to proclaim victory over sin and death itself. There Jesus preached the gospel to the righteous dead, those living under the law of Moses. (There is an additional school of theology that branches off, asserting that Jesus preached to all in hell, not just the righteous dead. And still others speculate whether he came to preach victory to those who were not righteous or to offer them good news.) This is the approach taken by C. S. Lewis through his allegory *The Lion, the Witch, and the Wardrobe*, in which Aslan frees statues created by the White Witch before a last great battle.

As you can see, there are a lot of questions and several viable options. While there are some strong ideas about what happened in hell/Sheol/Hades on that Holy Saturday, I believe it will remain a mystery until we ourselves are in heaven. That being said, when I am trying to understand a current question, I find it helpful to pull myself out of my current thinking and instead consider what the earliest generations would have thought or perhaps took for granted.

The earliest church fathers, the likes of Polycarp, Ignatius, Tertullian, and Augustine, along with pretty much all of the church's leaders until the Reformation in the sixteenth century, held a broadly unified understanding of what happened between the cross and the resurrection. As Matthew Emerson has noted: "The early Christian view of the descent is primarily understood as Jesus' journey to the place of the dead, his body in the grave and his soul in the place of the (righteous) dead, where he proclaims his victory over death and Hades."[1]

I have come to agree with the church fathers. I landed there by considering who I plan to see in heaven and how I account for that. Hebrews 12:22–23 explains that living believers have come to Mount Zion, and they are not alone. They join a festive gathering of

---

[1]Matthew Y. Emerson, *"He Descended to the Dead": An Evangelical Theology of Holy Saturday* (Downers Grove, IL: InterVarsity Press, 2019), 74–75.

angels, the church of the firstborn, and the spirits of the righteous made perfect. On what grounds, then, does this joyful proclamation of gathering with the generations stand?

The writer of Hebrews says the names of the firstborns (that is, Adam, Eve, Abraham, Sarah, Moses, etc.) have been written in heaven, and the righteous have now been made perfect. How do we account for the presence of those generations who were not perfect yet lived under the Law? They have been made perfect and can be found in heaven. How? Once I realized this was the question at hand, the answer (because I remembered God's character and promises) was apparent.

There was a rescue mission. That is what the wholly divine Christ did on Holy Saturday. He descended to the place of the dead for the first stop on his victory tour, rescuing the righteous, bearing freedom, grabbing the keys to Hades, and conquering death itself.

The question I want us to focus on is "How does this affect us today?" As we live through our Holy Saturdays, what lessons are we to carry with us?

We could get bogged down in the nuances of the theology, but I am going to challenge us all to instead hold on to the mystery and focus on what this has to do with us. I believe the simplest way to understand our response to Holy Saturday is when we take on the challenge of standing in the gap for others. This is what Jesus did for us, whether you understand his "descent" into hell as a metaphor or a literal action. In the same way, when we face a Holy Saturday—or those around us face trauma, death, or loss—we, too, are called to stand in the gap.

This means taking up a position of active, resolute defense for or against something. We will expose ourselves to potential harm as we seek to protect. We lift others so that they can rise above any assailing dangers. If someone falls, we are their support.[2]

Standing in the gap requires us to go through the breach in the proverbial city wall and fight for those who cannot fight for themselves. It is what happened on Holy Saturday, and it is what we are called to do as well.

Oftentimes, this may not look like literal actions of defense but, instead, a posture of intercessory prayer. That is, praying on behalf of someone else for God's mercy, for him to intercede. I have a friend who, when asked to pray for a situation, replies that she will be "storming heaven's gates." I love that visual.

How much more powerful is it when we are called to storm hell on behalf of a friend or loved one? Doing so with prayer is a call that we must heed. It is spiritual warfare, and it can be costly.

This is the other thing we must acknowledge as we stand in the gap. There is risk involved. Serving others like this, in prayer or in physical action, requires risk. Fighting for lives, for souls, comes at a cost. We go where we have no business being because they don't belong there either. I have had those moments in my life where I knew I was looking at the edge of hell and being asked to step in. It is humbling and scary. And the only courage and conviction I have when placed in that position is in recognizing that Christ did it first. I follow him, and he is the one who rescues. The mess and the muck don't need to scare us off. We can step into it knowing that being the one to stand in the gap is a profound honor and a total gift.

The beautiful truth that comes from all of this is that liberation is found when we face hell. When we stand in the gap, the place for subjugation is upended and, instead, freedom is found. We

---

[2] For an official dictionary definition of "To Stand in the Gap," see the Free Dictionary by Farlex, https://www.thefreedictionary.com/To+stand+in+the+gap.

are not the ones that can offer the true rescue we all need, but it is amazing to think that we get to be a part of that story for those we know when we stand in the gap. We get to witness liberation, and the celebration that eventually comes is so, so sweet.

Of all the celebrations we have at the lake, nothing quite compares to the whoops of glee that are screamed out the first time someone successfully water-skis. A jubilation erupts from us all as we witness the person rise up out of the water and fly across the lake.

To get to that point, though, someone must get right in the water with them. After the skis have been adjusted and they are securely attached, the skier leans back and attempts to shimmy their way into water deep enough for the skis to not hit the bottom. The helper, however, is forced to walk along with them, well past the swimming area that has been cleaned of debris, to the part of the lake where the bottom is full of decades of muck. Once there, the helper assists the skier by assuring proper form and communicating with the boat. While everyone else is on the shore, the helper is wet and dirty. Eventually, the go signal is given, and as the boat lunges forward, the skier seems to lift out of the water, only to crash down again. This can go on for several rounds, each time bringing the skier farther into the unknown.

This is when things get intense for the helper. The skier is well into the depths of the lake. The helper must swim out, get the skier reset with skis and rope, give them a pep talk, and oftentimes, pull them back to a more stable location. The helper, covered in muck and mire from chasing after the floundering skier and dragging them back to steady ground, no longer resists the reality that they, too, are swimming and, therefore, entirely soaking wet. All the while, those on the shore, dry and unscathed, watch the whole thing. But it is only the helper who knows how frustrated or tired or unsure the skier is, because it is the helper who goes out into the deep after them every time they fall down.

But then comes that moment when the helper yells out, "Hit it," and this time, the skier is lifted straight out of the deep and up to the surface of the water, and they are flying free across the lake. The beach erupts in cheers. And the helper swims back with dirty feet, holding on to their glasses or baseball cap as they make their way from the lake.

Everyone thinks that being the skier is the reward. But it is the helper, the one who braved the muck and depths and gave way to freedom, that has the greatest prize.

CHAPTER SEVEN

STILL WE GATHER

"Gather my saints together unto me." —Psalm 50:5 KJV

Down our long and very steep drive is a handful of cabins, ours counted among them, linked together for all of time it seems. An old rental colony turned into a home for us all. A haven. In the early 1980s, the cabins were bought by young professionals eager to have a place to escape the hustle and bustle of life. Of the handful, four of the cabins held young families that all grew up together. We are the Originals, the group of kids that joined together to create a roaming commune throughout the summer months.

The group we formed was unlike any group I have experienced. We had a wide age range and varying interests, yet we were glued together in a way that holds to this day. Something happens at the lake. Age no longer matters. The toddlers and the tweens play together in harmony. I would say it was a fluke, but we now see the same thing taking place with our own kids, the next generation, as they, too, claim the lake as their own.

The Originals would roam about, bouncing from cabin to cabin to beach and back again, throughout the days of summer. What we loved most of all was meeting at our forts. The forts were hangouts we built behind each cabin that we collectively worked on to claim as our own. Little patches of the forest that were just ours. We would gather and clear the sticks and branches, remove the rocks, set up logs as stools, and allow the towering pines to be the only structure required. But those forts, they were our gathering places. We held counsel there. We hashed out conflict there. We read or planned or rested for hours at a time. We lived there.

A few years ago, I took my kids on a tour of all the remnants of the forts from my youth. The forest had reclaimed them, for the most part. The sitting logs were knocked over. Branches had fallen into our meeting spaces. A deep bed of pine needles coated the ground. To the naked eye, they were underwhelming, easy to miss. But I could see the shadow of where we had gathered and lived. And it felt like we were all standing on sacred ground.

It wasn't the space or place that I was remembering. It was the living. The meetings at the forts, the stories told, the plans hatched, the truces made. It was all that happened as we gathered that caused the place to be sacred.

When we think of Jesus's followers in the time after his death, I think we tend to picture them scattered. While it is true they scattered, that's not the whole story. More importantly, it is not the story of what they did next.

What they did next was gather together.

When we look at the accounts of Matthew (28:8), Mark (16:7), and Luke (24:9), we see that the disciples were seemingly together by daybreak on Sunday. Since that is so, and the Sabbath would have prevented them from moving around too much, it makes sense that the disciples had gathered back together by the time of this next day, Holy Saturday.

As the Gospels continue on, it becomes apparent that the group has convened back in the upper room. We can't know for certain if that is where they gathered this next day, but it does seem evident that they had found their way back to each other. Luke tells us that the women on Sunday morning "reported all these things to the Eleven and to all the rest" (24:9). Matthew says the women "ran to tell his disciples" (28:8). The insinuation is that the disciples were together.

I think it is likely that they all gathered at John's house to begin with. While on the cross, Jesus entrusted his mom to John. "When Jesus saw his mother and the disciple he loved standing there, he said to his mother, 'Woman, here is your son.' Then he said to the disciple, 'Here is your mother.' And from that hour the disciple took her into his home" (John 19:26–27). Imagine Mary and John gathered together as one by one the disciples all make their way to the house. Perhaps as the house became too full, it was suggested they needed to move to the upper room.

However it happened, sometime between the hours of Good Friday and daybreak on Sunday, they found their way back together. This is remarkable.

Can you imagine the vulnerability and trust it would take to gather again after what had happened just hours before? They would be unable to hide the response they each displayed as they had denied or fled or scattered. To gather again required a turnaround, a humility, and most of all, an awareness that being together was better than being apart. The gathering was what led to wholeness.

It is from this place of gathering that they waited. Wondering what to do, seemingly practicing all the things we are reflecting on here: acknowledging what happened, remembering God's character, grieving, resting, holding peace, lamenting, and so it goes.

This gathering seemed essential as they experienced all that Holy Saturday and the days to come had for them. They were called to live the days together.

And this should be no surprise to us, because Jesus was serious about community, about living life together. This was his last lesson to the disciples throughout the Last Supper.[1] It is no accident that despite the chaos, the hurt, and the sadness of Good Friday, the disciples would come together again, and that their gathering would be around the Shabbat table as they experienced the meals that bring shalom.

This is not a gathering simply to have people around. This is not a buffer from reality made possible by a plethora of bodies as we can sometimes think we need, especially during those hard hours of waiting and wondering or of grieving and confusion. No, this is being known and seen deeply. Gathering with those from whom you cannot hide, that is where you find comfort as you grieve, lament, rest.

> There is immeasurable trust and comfort. You are truly known and seen and loved for exactly who you are. There is freedom in friendship like that, just as there is freedom within Christ himself who knows you and sees you and loves you for who you are. The freedom is breathtaking. It allows you to open yourself up and sacrifice yourself. It allows you to forgive and repent. It allows you to break bread together, with grace and love and mercy, understanding and compassion.[2]

---

[1] For more study on community and the Last Supper, see Jessica Herberger, *Break Bread Together: Finding True Friendship at the Last Supper* (Abilene, TX: Leafwood, 2020).

[2] Herberger, *Break Bread Together*, 178.

To have that kind of community you must live life together, up close and without pretense. I think this is perhaps one of the reasons our community at the lake is so close. It isn't the amount of time or even the frequency of time spent together, it is the life lived in close proximity with no facade. There is no ability to pretend you are anything other than yourself, because we know each other for having lived side by side with each other. Imagine how much trust it takes to take a vacation with another family. Now imagine the vacation lasts most of the summer and you share a beach and your houses are all within earshot of each other. These people know me. They remember who I was at age five, ten, fifteen, twenty, and so on. They see me in my kids as they read or sass or swim their hearts out because they knew me as a kid. We know how we act when we are mad at each other or a spouse or a parent. Life lived, over decades, together and up close, creates an understanding and a connection that is divinely deep. This type of gathering of the saints must mark the church since our world is experiencing an ongoing and ever-increasing epidemic of loneliness.

Dietrich Bonhoeffer formed a small community of seminary students who were training to become ministers in a hard age. They lived life together through two challenging years until the gestapo closed their doors permanently. Two of Bonhoeffer's students, Gerhard Müller and Albrecht Schönherr, survived and give testimony to how Christian community can edify and transform our ever-changing world:

> As a post-Christian society develops, the various forms of community life in the local congregation and in the larger church take on especially increasing significance as intensive means by which to encounter the sources of Christian life in Word, sacrament, and faithful life in community. They fortify the Christian, who is

> threatened with isolation, to proclaim the gospel and to take an active part in the autonomous life of society in the Spirit of Christ.[3]

In a world of superficial relationships and fluctuating community, the church must be an example of another way to live.

When we gather, we must, literally, open the door for others. The opening of a door is a sign of welcome. What was Peter thinking as he opened the door? What type of courage and humility did it require? Or perhaps more accurately, what depth of desperation would propel him to show up again? To return to the gathering after having fallen, denying Jesus as Peter did being just one example, is an act of faith.

What community do you go to when it all seems to have fallen apart?

Who do you go to when you are the one that had a hand in the destruction?

Who do we go to when living the life before us feels impossible?

I imagine the words ringing in Peter's ears as he faced the door, behind which his community was gathering, were something like, "Where else could I go?" When things got tough for the twelve during their ministry with Jesus, they realized the answer to that question. There was a time when Jesus was losing disciples in response to his teaching. They called the teaching difficult, saying it was unacceptable. The twelve, also confused by the teaching, were then asked if they, too, wanted to turn away. Peter answered for the group when he said: "Lord, to whom will we go? You have the words of eternal life. We have come to believe and know that you are the Holy One of God" (John 6:68–69).

---

[3] Gerhard Müller and Albrecht Schönherr, "Afterword," in *Life Together and Prayerbook of the Bible*, vol. 5 of Dietrich Bonhoeffer's *Works* (Minneapolis: Fortress Press, 1996), 139–40.

When all seems lost, still we gather. We head home. As Peter said, where else could we ever want to go? On Holy Saturday, Peter lived this out.

Gatherings that reflect Jesus must reflect this need to return to our true home. They extend a greeting with warmth and delight, a true welcome. This is the church, gathering as Jesus would have us. When Jesus said we would have trouble in the world (John 16:33), I wonder if he was talking not just about external trouble but also internal trouble. We will fall; we will doubt; we will mess up. And yet, Jesus also promised us peace. The peace he promised is found in him. The word used in Scripture is *eirēnē*, and this is a peace that comes from joining together. Peace is found when we join with Jesus, yes, but also when we gather together in the midst of our trouble, internal or external. Gathering together sets the table for peace.

When we have trouble of any kind, we can easily convince ourselves that the answer is isolation. While there is certainly a beauty in the quiet aloneness, retreating to solitude is not the path to peace when there is trouble. We can find wholeness in joining together, welcoming each other with open arms, no matter the trouble we all find ourselves in.

As I speak to more and more people who are deconstructing or examining their faith, I find that the first step to returning to church is the yearning to gather. That is the turnaround. When looking at the rubble of their faith, sorting out what to hold on to, what to let go of, and where to begin rebuilding, the first step back is to regather. How do we welcome them? I fear our response is not always as warm and open as it is called to be. I wonder if we could all be more like those disciples as they greeted each other that Holy Saturday when we welcome each other back into gathering today.

Not to belabor the point, but let's consider again what it means that this gathering was happening on Sabbath. The day of shalom.

The meals of shalom. The table beckoning them to sit and find the peace their souls were craving. This is what happens as we gather. We find shalom and then can be shalom in the world.

Here sit those first believers. The forebearers of our faith. Hurt, confused, ashamed, and yet still, they gathered. The church today has much to learn from them. The gathering of the saints is so much more than a worship service on Sunday. It is far more simple and far deeper than what we call church today. Gathering, as we see it on Holy Saturday, is radical vulnerability, humility, welcome, and reconciliation.

Known. Loved. Welcomed. Filled with shalom. Gathered.

It is from that place that we can, together, grieve, lament, rest, and carry on in this in-between we all find ourselves in.

In the corner of the screened porch is possibly the world's ugliest table. It is a leftover from my dad's bachelor apartment. Said apartment was furnished in 1980 with furniture from the mid-1970s. My mom called it his "Man of La Mancha" phase. The wood is dark and heavy. The legs of the table are six inches wide, and they curve at odd angles. The tabletop is a rough octagon. The words are not doing justice to how unseemly the thing is. But there it sits. And despite its appearance, it is loved.

That table in the corner of our screened porch has been witness to and the bearer of so much living. Gathered around that table, the Originals have played countless hours of cards. Gathered around that table, thousands of meals have been enjoyed. Dinners that start after the sunset and carry on late into the night. Morning coffees, afternoon projects, puzzles and paintings, fishing pole repairs, all at that table.

Above the table hangs a tiffany lamp, stained glass with grapes and grapevines weaving through the shards. Based on the pure look of it, the lampshade is too beautiful for the table. Yet in a decision that must have been inspired, my mom hung it right there, and it all makes sense together. That beautiful lamp hanging over that unsightly table as if the lamp itself knew what beauty would happen *around* the table. Just like mosquitos seek the golden glow of the tiffany lamp, we all flock to that table.

That table holds some of my happiest memories and so much of my life. Just like the table itself, we can show up with all our flaws and be welcomed, known, loved. The wholeness we find as we gather together again at the lake is so profound because it points to the wholeness of shalom. This is the church. The gathering of the saints, the open door, the welcoming of our return again and again, flaws and all, to find shalom and be shalom in the world.

PART THREE

CHAPTER EIGHT

KEEP WATCH

"I wait for the Lord
more than watchmen for the morning—
more than watchmen for the morning." —Psalm 130:6

Our little colony of cabins has a community beach we all share. In our family, we call it "the big beach," which speaks to its size only in comparison to the beach we have in front of our own cabin. The big beach is where a lot of our communal life gets lived out. This is beautifully evident once the swimming area is full of children because there is always an adult with eyes on the water.

The swimming area is roped off with a scratchy nylon rope that, as the years go by, gets coarser and coarser. The rope runs through a floating buoy every three feet or so. Together they form a rectangle of safety jutting off the shore of the beach, keeping boaters at bay and children contained. At the back of the swimming area is a floating raft. The raft is yellow; it has been since I first showed up at Paradox in 1983, except for the dismal few years in the early 2000s when we had a silver aluminum raft.

When I was the generation of children swimming to the raft, it was a wooden concoction floating on Styrofoam blocks. The raft was a yellow point in the otherwise blue-and-green landscape of an Adirondack lake surrounded by mountains. It was our freedom as kids. We could hole up on that yellow island for hours, reading, talking, jumping off, and swimming under the raft. For a time, we had switched out to the aluminum monster. That raft rested on pontoons and allowed for a much, much safer journey for those brave enough to swim under it. Thanks be to God, our community bought a new raft recently, and it is yellow, as it ought to be. All that to say, I want you to picture a yellow raft as you picture the watchers on the beach.

The adults on the beach always have a designated water watcher. This is the adult who says, *I won't read my book or get engrossed in conversation, instead, I will watch.* It's a serious job, and those words, "I'll watch," are said with great reverence. They mean you are ready to intercede should something happen and that you are constantly doing a head count in the water. "Who's behind the raft?!" is a constant thought for the watcher.

As the child in the water, I thought nothing of this arrangement. I truly took for granted the fact that anyone was even keeping tabs on us as we bobbed up and down in the water and waves. That all changed when my own kids were old enough and brave enough to swim to the raft. Suddenly, the role of watcher was critical.

As the kids have grown to be stronger and stronger swimmers over the years, there is always a bit of back-and-forth about the actual need for a watcher.

"Can we go swimming at the big beach?"

"Yes, but who is down there to watch?"

"We will be fine! We are good swimmers."

"There must be an adult watching. You cannot keep watch over yourselves."

They are as obtuse as I was about the need, value, and necessity of the watchman.

Last summer, there was a day on our quiet lake that was disrupted by a pair of wild jet skiers. Our small lake is no place for anyone looking to go really fast, because there are simply not enough miles from shore to shore to make that happen. But these guys were intent on getting as much speed as they could. I have no idea what possessed them, but they came flying across the lake at full throttle right toward the back of the raft. My friend and I, the watchers of the day, jumped up with arms waving, yelling for them to stop and redirect. They came within a few feet of the raft. The jet skiers had no idea there were kids right there. And the kids had no idea they were in peril. It took the watchers.

Most of the time, keeping watch on the beach is a pretty boring post. More than anything, it is a sign of the utmost trust between all of us adults that we pass the post to each other. Trusting someone else when your kids are in the water is a level of confidence in another that is hard to find. Yet we have it there. History and relationship and decades of knowing each other allows us the freedom to relinquish our post to another. To hear another say "I'll watch" and know that what they are really saying is, "All is well; I will guard and protect and tend and keep your own as if they are mine, because to me, they are. They are mine." And then to believe that in your soul? It is rare and beautiful.

What would it look like to keep watch, to be a watchman on Holy Saturday? The followers of Jesus were waiting. And the ones who were waiting with hope were the watchmen. The ones who paid attention to their circumstances (as discussed in Chapter One) and remembered their history (which we talked about in Chapter Two) were able to be true watchmen. Not just for themselves but, I imagine, for each other as well.

Watchmen were traditionally found at the edges of the city, looking out. In fact, the word means to lean forward and behold. Watchmen would look for enemies or trouble approaching, but they would also be looking for friends in the distance. Watchmen often were the sentinels, announcing the rising of the sun or the dawn of a new day. Watchmen would not leave their posts. They were steady, faithful, eyes ever peeled. Waiting.

Let's not forget this was Passover week in Jerusalem. The pilgrims, including the disciples and the other followers of Jesus, who traveled into Jerusalem would have been singing those Songs of Ascent that are a group of psalms (120–34) traditionally sung as travelers made their way to Jerusalem for the major festivals of Unleavened Bread (Passover), Weeks, and Tabernacles. These songs would have been fresh on everyone's mind as they waited on that Sabbath.

> I wait for the LORD; I wait
> and put my hope in his word.
> I wait for the Lord
> more than watchmen for the morning—
> more than watchmen for the morning.
> Israel, put your hope in the LORD.
> For there is faithful love with the LORD,
> and with him is redemption in abundance. (Ps. 130:5–7)

Waiting, watching, with a hope and devotion stronger even than the watchmen on the towers of the city. This is the call of Psalm 130. This psalm is titled "Awaiting Redemption," and goodness, if that doesn't perfectly describe Holy Saturday. Keeping watch while holding on to the Lord is the posture that allows us to hold each other up in hope.

Less than twenty-four hours before his death, Jesus himself called the disciples to keep watch. As he was in the garden of Gethsemane, Jesus directed them to "watch and pray so that you will not fall into temptation," explaining that "the spirit is willing, but the flesh is weak" (Mark 14:38 NIV). While Jesus was "grieved to the point of death" (Mark 14:34), he told the disciples, more than once, to keep watching.

We must not miss that Jesus even told them *why* it was important. "So that you won't enter into temptation." The disciples were tasked with keeping watch as Jesus prayed so that *they* would have a well of strength to draw from when they needed it. Keeping watch over others blesses us. It strengthens our hope, and it fills the well we will need to draw from.

But as we know, keeping watch is hard. It is so much easier to look away than to stay steady. We don't know how to handle discomfort. Have you ever seen someone grieving to the point of death? "My soul is overwhelmed with sorrow to the point of death. . . . Stay here and keep watch" (Mark 14:34 NIV). To watch someone grieve like that is painful. It is messy. The wailing, or that dreadful silent moan as they cannot even make a sound. The red face, the shaking, the snotty nose, and the bloodshot eyes. It is a brutal sight. So often our response to that kind of grief, or any discomfort, is to give the person privacy and space.

"Take a minute and pull yourself together."

"Let's find you a quiet spot where you can be alone."

At funerals, the grieving mother gets ushered away by a well-meaning family member. As a friend falls apart, we may lay a hand on their back, but we avert our eyes. We are programmed to minimize discomfort, and when someone is so undone that they are offering a display of what it looks like to struggle, we do our best to reclaim our own comfort by looking away.

Yet how much we lose in averting our eyes.

Go back to Jesus's words to the disciples. Keeping watch over another is for our good. If we can face the discomfort found in watching another's discomfort, not gawking but rather truly seeing, standing watch, we are blessed. And so are they.

Conversely, the answer to our weakness is having others keeping watch over us. When we are lost, hopeless, drowning, the answer is that we need watchmen and we need to be watchmen. But if I am being honest, I do not want anyone to see me in my weakness. I find my own private corner. I hide myself away.

Similar to the drawing away that happens when we forsake gathering, grieving in solitude appears easier than inviting others to keep watch on our behalf. Were it not for those words of Jesus in the garden of Gethsemane, pressing the disciples to keep watch as he grieved, I might find a way to justify my response. The truth is, I think it will be too painful for me to be seen and known in the depths of my grief. Yet Jesus demonstrates that we can trust others to keep watch. And not only that, it is as good for them as it is for us. This is a lesson I have been learning slowly, a truth I am starting to believe after many, many years of grieving on my own.

Earlier this year, my daughter and I were driving home after a few errands. She was singing along to some soft rock, laughing and smiling. All of a sudden, a wave of grief came crashing around me. How much she is like my mom, her grandma she has never met. How much my mom would adore this young lady. How much I wished my mom was in the car with us, singing along. I could barely breathe. When we pulled into the driveway, I told her to go on in the house because I needed to do something before following. I held it together until I was alone in my car, and then I broke down.

It was the kind of wave that catches you off guard and literally knocks the wind out of you. And it all came. That dreadful silent moan as I could not even make a sound. The red face, the shaking, the snotty nose, and the bloodshot eyes. I texted Josh. "Please come see me outside." He raced outside and later told me that as he looked into the car, he thought I was having a heart attack. That's how brutal grief can look. I lowered the window as he was ready to call 911, and he asked, "Do you need help?"

"I am okay," I said as I relayed the story of the wave that caught me off guard. "I knew I needed you here." We have been doing the grief thing for long enough, fifteen years now, that he knew what to do. And he stood watch. He didn't look away. He didn't minimize it or try to make it better.

After a few minutes, I nodded my head, exhaled, and looked at him. I was ready to get up and face the rest of the day. The grief had dissipated to almost nothing. As swiftly and surely as it arrived, it fled. Josh told me he was glad I texted, that I did not hide or stay in the car alone. Fifteen years of learning what works and what doesn't, yet it still requires an act of faith and vulnerability for me to say, "Come. Keep watch."

That's the tension. The Paradox. We want to be independent like my young teenagers, sure of our strength and ability, especially within the safety of the boundaries set before us. But we cannot keep watch over ourselves. We need someone on the shore with eyes that can guard and preserve. We need watchmen. And we need to be watchmen for those we love.

If we are able to combine the forward-facing, hopeful waiting of the watchmen with the steady presence of those who keep watch, we can experience hope and peace in the waiting. It takes the watchmen to say all will be well. It takes one who does not look away to allow us to be known and seen and blessed as we grieve.

One quiet August day a few summers ago, my friend, one of the Originals, was on the big beach watching our two daughters out on the raft. It was rare for him to be at the lake. His adulthood was a hard one, and more often than not, an entire summer would go by without seeing him. But that weekend found us there together, and I am forever grateful for it, as it was the last time I would see him.

On that quiet August day, he had dragged an Adirondack chair out of the long line of them that stood guard at the back of the beach, facing the edge of the shore. And there he sat, keeping watch over our girls, who were doing exactly what we had done at their age a few decades earlier. Standing on my front deck, I could hear the girls but only see him at his post along the shore.

Something in me knew this was a moment I did not want to miss, so I headed down to the beach to join him. I, too, dragged a chair from the formation, carving a trail in the sand as I settled in next to him at the shore. He smiled and pointed at the girls as we once again marveled at the timelessness of this place. His eyes never left the girls as he kept watch. But my post that day was with him. Watching and noticing the fully present peace that was in him and around him in those moments. A peace that so often eluded. I saw it. And in the watching, that peace was preserved and passed on in moments of grief that followed in the months to come. But that day, I watched him as he watched the girls, and we were both blessed by our watching.

CHAPTER NINE

TRUST GOD IS WORKING

"In his defense Jesus said to them, 'My Father is always at his work to this very day, and I too am working.'"
—John 5:17 NIV

Paradox Lake, because of its namesake (the paradox of water running back into the lake from what is supposed to be an outlet), is a lake of fluctuating water levels. After a rainy spring, or even after a decent rainstorm, there will be a day or so when the water reverses and the level rises. There have been a few times when our little beach went underwater overnight due to the rising water levels. Our beach, the little one in front of our house that is surrounded by trees, becomes a lagoon. Paradoxes can be fun, the beach becoming a lagoon a novel thing, and usually, before we know it, the water is back to how it is supposed to be. The water running both ways was displayed most dramatically, however, when Hurricane Irene landed in the mountains of upstate New York in 2011.

That summer, Irene had snaked its way from the Caribbean to North Carolina, but we were on our little beach, thinking the storm would never make it all the way into the Adirondack Park. And if it did, we expected our little beach to perhaps be underwater a bit and create a lagoon. The rain might spoil some of our fun and make packing the car to head home a bit of a struggle, but that is about as far as we thought it would go.

We were wrong.

Jesus's words in Matthew 7:25, "The rain fell, the rivers rose, and the winds blew and pounded the house," seemed to accurately describe of the onset of Hurricane Irene in upstate New York. We had most definitely underestimated the storm. By the time the rain had slowed to a drizzle the next day, we looked out on a beach fully submerged. In addition, there was a paradox so that, while the rain had ceased, the level of the lake was rising more swiftly than we had ever seen. The sheer volume of water pouring into our lake was hard to comprehend. Here are some specifics from a nearby river to give perspective on what was happening:

> A U.S. Geological Survey river gauge near Au Sable Forks recorded the river's discharge rate—a measure of the volume of water flowing in the river—at just over 200 cubic feet per second, near the 90-year median flow rate at the site. After moderate rainstorms on Thursday, the gauge measured near 3,000 cubic feet per second. During spring high-water levels, when snowmelt pulses through the watershed, the gauge may measure flows of around 12,000 cubic feet per second. During Irene, the gauge topped out at a whopping 50,000 cubic feet per second.[1]

---

[1]Zachary Matson, "Irene 10 Years Later: Adirondacks Still Bear Scars of 'Perfect Storm,'" *The Daily Gazette*, September 1, 2021, https://dailygazette.com/2021/08/24/irene-10-years-later-adirondacks-still-bear-scars-of-perfect-storm/.

There was a 25,000 percent increase in water.

The influx of water into our lake seemed to have no end. We watched as chairs we had sat on just the day before were covered in four, five, six feet of water. Even when the rain had stopped, the waters continued to run backward, *into* the lake.

Irene had, with her fierce winds, knocked down several large trees on the driveway which meant we could not leave. We were stuck. And still the water rose. *When will it end?* I wondered. *How* will it end? Is it even possible for this to be undone? I felt so unsettled as creation was upended all around me.

Waiting and watching the waterline became my full-time mission. The water level at our shore crested our beach and moved up onto our stairs, then it overtook a whole section of steps coming up to the landing. The big beach was fully submerged as well. Water lapped against the retaining wall as if it were the ocean. This was unprecedented.

The following day, two days after the storm landed on our haven, the water levels still held. The paradox would continue until the levels receded in the water bodies further south. Bit by bit, far out of sight, the water began flowing south again. Sure enough, eventually, the Schroon River gave way and the water flow corrected. The outlet of Paradox Lake was once again an outlet.

The undoing, the storm that turned it all backward, happened in a flash. Righting the waters took much longer. Yet there was an undercurrent working the whole time, fixing all that was upended.

I try to remember this every time we see a paradox. We may wake up to a reduced beach or the waves headed in a different direction. It can be disorienting. How could it change so fast and, more importantly, when will it be fixed? It may look like nothing is happening to right the upending. Yet this truth remains: all will be made well as God continues to work.

Holy Saturday looks like a blank pause in the midst of the work of Holy Week. At first glance, it can appear as if it is a day of nothingness. While it was, on the surface, a day of quiet, it was not a day of inaction. How often do we perceive quiet as inaction? Yet God is continuously at work. Even in the quiet of Holy Saturday, Christ was fulfilling prophecy, proclaiming liberation, all for our good.

There was likely a sense of abandonment that day. Those same questions I asked as I looked out at the rising waters reflected in the confusion of God's seeming silence. But just as I could not see the waters receding for days, there was time yet before the full power of the restoration bought on the cross could be made apparent to those watching. What felt like, and even looked like, desertion was not the whole picture of what was happening.

When things are upended, we look for help. And when we don't see restoration coming at the time we expect, it is easy to become frustrated, hopeless, or angry. We start asking questions. How can this be undone? What will it take to right the wrong? As the questions flood your mind, know that you are in good company. Listen to the words of King David:

> How long, LORD? Will you forget me forever?
> How long will you hide your face from me?
> How long will I store up anxious concerns within me,
> agony in my mind every day?
> How long will my enemy dominate me?
> Consider me and answer, LORD my God.
> Restore brightness to my eyes;
> otherwise, I will sleep in death.
> My enemy will say, "I have triumphed over him,"
> and my foes will rejoice because I am shaken.

> But I have trusted in your faithful love;
> my heart will rejoice in your deliverance.
> I will sing to the Lord
> because he has treated me generously. (Ps. 13:1–6)

The questions of verses 1 and 2 in particular are the questions of someone who doesn't see God moving on their behalf. These are the questions of someone who sees or is living through an upending and wants to know how it could possibly be righted.

When we can't discern where or how God is working, our response is often just like David's. We question. This is normal. We see only the surface of what is happening, and often, from the surface, it doesn't look like things are turning for the better. But look what happens in verse 5. "I have trusted."

What is David trusting in?

It is the unceasing work of God on our behalf. Psalm 13 reminds us that even when we have unanswered questions, we can trust in God to treat us generously. This is living by faith in the face of death, floods, upendings of any kind. We question in our humanness; we trust by faith.

Trusting that God is always working emboldens our faith. Trusting that God's story, the bigger story, is working for good, even when our current reality seems impossible, is what sets aside the heroes of our faith. In Hebrews 11 we see story after story of faithfulness demonstrated as a trust in God despite the immediate circumstances. Abraham and Sarah stand out as amazing examples of this. Abraham remained fixed on God's reality, not his own, and from there, his faith held. Abraham held on to belief that he would have even one child, never mind father a nation of believers, belief that God would stay true to his promises and birth a nation through Isaac, even amid preparing to sacrifice that son, belief that God's plan for his life was good.

When we are faced with the same disconnect between an impossible current reality and the hope of God, we get to remember that God is always working for our good. We can find comfort in knowing his unceasing work toward that end. We grow tired; we lose interest; we doubt; we question. But God is steadfast. He does not abandon his post, no matter what it looks like from the surface.

This is what Psalm 121, another Song of Ascent, speaks directly to. The Lord is trustworthy. He will not stop. He does not stop. And in that reality, we find peace.

Psalm 121
The Lord Our Protector
A song of ascents.

I lift my eyes toward the mountains.
Where will my help come from?
My help comes from the LORD,
the Maker of heaven and earth.
He will not allow your foot to slip;
your Protector will not slumber.
Indeed, the Protector of Israel
does not slumber or sleep.
The LORD protects you;
the LORD is a shelter right by your side.
The sun will not strike you by day
or the moon by night.
The LORD will protect you from all harm;
he will protect your life.
The LORD will protect your coming and going
both now and forever.

It is the constancy of Psalm 121 that brings me the most comfort. God will not slumber or sleep; he continues. There is no weariness on God's part. I don't think we have the ability to truly, fully understand this. We are so drawn to the immediate that when the immediate looks like silence, we feel disoriented. From there it is quite easy to imagine that God has abandoned us. We are fickle; we are easily distracted; we are always falling short, and so it makes sense to us that God might throw up his hands in frustration and leave us to our own devices.

Nothing is further from the truth.

His faithfulness endures. And we can count on that even when we can't see it.

Eugene Peterson, in *A Long Obedience in the Same Direction*, writes,

> The only serious mistake we can make when illness comes, when anxiety threatens, when conflict disturbs our relationships with others is to conclude that God has gotten bored looking after us and has shifted his attention to a more exciting Christian, or that God has become disgusted with our meandering obedience and decided to let us fend for ourselves for a while, or that God has gotten too busy fulfilling prophecy in the Middle East to take time now to sort out the complicated mess we have gotten ourselves into. That is the only serious mistake we can make. It is the mistake that Psalm 121 prevents: the mistake of supposing that God's interest in us waxes and wanes in response to our spiritual temperature.[2]

There is no "off the job" for God. We must remember this, especially when we don't see signs of action. More often than not,

---

[2] Eugene H. Peterson, *A Long Obedience in the Same Direction: Discipleship in an Instant Society* (1980, reprint, Downers Grove, IL: InterVarsity Press, 2020), 37–38.

the moving is not what or how or when we would have planned. But this does not negate the constant working of God for our good.

As we know, the trials will come. The waters will rise, loved ones will perish, relationships will break. Yet we can trust that the work of God continues. There are times when God uses our circumstances, and there are times when God works under or around our circumstances. Our call is to hold fast and to trust. Again, Peterson is helpful here: "The promise of the psalm—and both Hebrews and Christians have always read it this way—is not that we shall never stub our toes but that no injury, no illness, no accident, no distress will have evil power over us, that is, will be able to separate us from God's purpose in us."[3]

The work of the Christian is to exercise faith in the dark, in the quiet, in the confusion. To do that, we must adjust our eyesight and look below the surface. We must zoom way out and remember the bigness of God's story. We must wait.

To trust in God's continuous working is to wait on the Lord. To believe all will be well, to trust that, even when we can't see it, is the work of the believer. This type of trust takes courage. In my times of greatest unknown, I have recited, again and again, the words of Psalm 27:13–14 (NIV):

> I remain confident of this:
>   I will see the goodness of the LORD
>   in the land of the living.
> Wait for the LORD;
>   be strong and take heart
>   and wait for the LORD.

We can be confident. Our trusting will not make us fools. Take heart, when the waters rise, when even the paradoxes are turned

---

[3] Peterson, *A Long Obedience in the Same Direction*, 36.

upside down, we can find comfort in trusting that the God who loves us never stops working. Peace is found when we do.

Paradox, besides being a lake of perplexing water movement, is also a spring-fed lake. This means underground springs feed the lake from the bottom with fresh, clean mountain water rather than having an inlet as the lake's water source. This results in a beautifully clear and very healthy lake. Where some lakes can have cloudy water, algae problems, even a smell, spring-fed lakes are blessed with crystal clear water and no stagnation. Spring-fed lakes are also cold.

The springs supply the lake with the coldest of water, and even if the lake temperature tends to balance out, the springs themselves are downright frosty. These jets of water shooting up from the water table below the lake are invisible from the surface. Yet as you swim through one, you can for sure feel it. The biting cold of a spring can take your breath away.

Imagine swimming through an unseen vertical stream of icy water. That's what it's like when you find a spring in the lake. From the top of the water, there is no indication of springs feeding the lake. There is never a ripple to prepare you for the burst of cold. You can't predict where they are, because they burst forth through the bottom of the lake at constantly changing locations.

Many times, I have been swimming with a friend who unknowingly swims through a spring. "What was that?!" they inevitably exclaim, the icy water shocking them as they pass through. I assure them all is well and fill them in on the source of our lake's water. I tell them it's why the lake is so clean and the fishing is so good, why there aren't too many slimy plants. The springs, which we never see, are always working.

Clean, fresh water coming into the lake. We never see it, we sometimes feel it, but we benefit from it all the time. The springs are constantly working.

> See, I am doing a new thing!
> Now it springs up; do you not perceive it?
> I am making a way in the wilderness
> and streams in the wasteland.
> The wild animals honor me,
> the jackals and the owls,
> because I provide water in the wilderness
> and streams in the wasteland,
> to give drink to my people, my chosen,
> the people I formed for myself
> that they may proclaim my praise.
> (Isa. 43:19–21 NIV)

When I read the prophet's words, I picture the springs in the lake—causing thriving, yet remaining unseen. They remind me of God, working for our good, providing for his people, deserving of praise, and worthy of our trust.

CHAPTER TEN

WELCOME LONG-SUFFERING

"But thou, O Lord, art a God full of compassion, and gracious, longsuffering, and plenteous in mercy and truth." —Psalm 86:15 KJV

When the fog is thick, or the sun is setting, I slip my kayak into the water and chase the loon. The loons tend to like the water in one specific area of the lake, and so I can usually find one somewhere between the shores to the right of our beach and the peninsula across the way. I glide out to the middle and wait. Seemingly out of nowhere, the loon will pop up its head, and I see that unmistakable profile. I head in his direction, determined to get as close as possible while not upsetting him. As I paddle his way, he dives into the water without so much as a splash. I know what this means. The waiting begins.

Loons are exceptional divers and underwater swimmers. Unlike most birds, their bones are solid (versus hollow) causing them to sink more swiftly and with greater ease. The loons can plunge to depths of over two hundred feet and hold their breath for five minutes. They dive deep, they swim far, and it is impossible to know when they will breach the surface of the lake once they do.

To wait for a loon to resurface is to exercise patience.

I sit in the kayak, the paddle across my lap, scanning the lake to see where he might pop up. I know enough to know I have no idea where that might be. I remain amazed at their endurance and the ease with which they withstand the underwater conditions.

Waiting, waiting. I begin to get frustrated. And perhaps a bit hopeless. Confident I have missed my chance to see him, I huff and puff a bit.

And then, as nonchalantly as he disappeared, he is there. And at once I recognize how impatient I really am and how long the arc of time is.

I'm not sure we talk about patience enough when we speak about grief. I wonder if this points to our intense desire to get beyond grief in a way that is simply unrealistic and wholly unhealthy. Or perhaps it points to our cultural need to appear strong, pulled together, unflappable. So we avoid grief, push it aside or shove it down, reject it as the uninvited intruder it is.

What if, instead, we welcome the long-suffering nature of grief? Rather than avoid it, we could recognize that to grieve is a sign of having loved.

Theologian N. T. Wright shared this insight in his book *God and the Pandemic*:

> Grief, after all is part of love. Not to grieve, not to lament, is to slam the door on the same place in the innermost heart from which love itself comes. Our

> culture is afraid of grief, but not just because it is afraid of death. That is natural and normal, a proper reaction to the Last Enemy. Our culture is afraid because it seems to be afraid of the fear itself, frightened that even to name grief will be to collapse forever. We have to keep going we tell ourselves, we have to be strong. Well, yes. Strong like Jesus who wept at the tomb of his friend.[1]

This is so important for us to remember. Jesus could have easily skipped past grieving for Lazarus, but he did not. To welcome grief is the decision of the wise, the strong. If Jesus chose to welcome grief, so must we. I imagine this was more natural to do in the first century because their culture was more comfortable with discomfort, more intimately acquainted with death, and probably more likely to welcome the concept of long-suffering in grief.

We much prefer to move through the motions, to get through something and put grief behind us. I am guilty of this to the highest order. Yet grief flies in the face of such sensibilities.

A few months after my mother died, I began to wrestle with this notion as I realized that the death of my mother wasn't going to be something I could "get over." This was a shocking revelation to me. The grief was a part of me. While I know now, fifteen years later, that it is not always the headline story of my life, the grief, nevertheless, has stayed.

I appreciate so much how Amanda Held Opelt writes,

> All grief is chronic to some degree. Nothing fills the void of the person you lost. Contrary to popular belief, having a baby does not mentally and emotionally undo

---

[1] N. T. Wright, *God and the Pandemic: A Christian Reflection on the Coronavirus and Its Aftermath* (Grand Rapids: Zondervan Reflective, 2020), 53.

> a previous miscarriage. Making new friends does not lessen the pain of losing a friend. Remarrying does not replace the deceased spouse. There is no "recovery" from that kind of pain.[2]

If there is no getting over grief, then patience is required. Patience with ourselves as we grieve and patience with those we love as they grieve. We need more voices in the church proclaiming this truth. Imagine if the church could be the place where there is space for those who grieve to not feel rushed out of their grieving?

When we slow down, welcome grief, and give ourselves patience, we are allowing the work of long-suffering to root down into our lives. This is good work for the Christian. Long-suffering is how David describes God in Psalm 86, "But thou, O Lord, art a God full of compassion, and gracious, longsuffering, and plenteous in mercy and truth" (v. 15 KJV). David was using the way God described himself to Moses in Exodus as inspiration here, "And the LORD passed by before him, and proclaimed, The LORD, The LORD God, merciful and gracious, longsuffering, and abundant in goodness and truth" (Exod. 34:6 KJV).

Both scriptures list long-suffering as a positive attribute. Look at the words that surround long-suffering in both instances as well: merciful, gracious, abundant, full of compassion, and plenteous. To consider that all those words have anything to do with long-suffering is particularly challenging to my modern mind.

What if welcoming long-suffering brings with it all those other things? Surely goodness, mercy, abundance, and compassion are a balm to those who are grieving. I wonder if in our haste to push through grief we miss the opportunity to be comforted in exactly the way the Lord designed.

---

[2] Amanda Held Opelt, *A Hole in the World: Finding Hope in Rituals of Grief and Healing* (New York: Worthy, 2022), 148–49.

Could it be that when we welcome the long-suffering grief requires of us rather than push it aside, we suffer less? Certainly, that has been the case for me.

The additional griefs I have faced after accepting that grief is in fact chronic, as Opelt said, have been full of so much mercy, goodness, and compassion. I have been able to go easy on myself, to have patience with myself as I faced subsequent losses. Where before I felt frustration when waves of sadness would crash, I now know this is just part of what happens and to be generous with myself. This posture has allowed me to extend mercy and compassion to those I know who are also grieving. When a loved one knows their grief is welcome with you and will be met with patience, they experience gracious and abundant love. Replacing the idea of a finish line with a posture of patience is what makes all the difference.

This is a countercultural way of handling grief. Rather than consider grief to be something we absorb into our reality, something we endure, we are often taught that it is something to be overcome. I imagine we will never fully understand the effects of Elisabeth Kübler-Ross and her work in *On Death & Dying*. While professionals have largely stepped away from her five stages of grief, it seems the concept of a finish line to grief has nonetheless woven itself into our vernacular and, therefore, our own expectations.

What we experience in grief does not align with those expectations. And because of that dissonance, we are often left shocked by our own grief. Michelle Zauner describes that disconnect in her beautiful and raw memoir on losing and grieving her own mother, *Crying in H Mart*. "Sometimes my grief feels as though I've been left alone in a room with no doors. Every time I remember that my mother is dead, it feels like I'm colliding with a wall that won't give. There's no escape, just a hard surface that I keep ramming into over and over, a reminder of the immutable reality that I will never see her again."[3]

It seems that acknowledging this cultural expectation will help us settle in to the grief given to us rather than rage against it or shove it aside. We realize that to hold on to grief is to work against what we are taught in the world. Patience is required. To be clear, grief comes from all sorts of things. From the passing of a loved one, yes, but also the death of a dream, loss of an opportunity, or the end of a relationship.

Our desire to be over it, whatever the *it* is, does not align with the life of one who follows Jesus. Instead, we get to welcome the long-suffering and, with it, the comfort of God himself.

I do think that Kübler-Ross was right in that a measure of acceptance is required. Accepting that the path laid before us will include grief. Endurance is necessary. We must continue on living while holding on to the reality of our grief.

There is time for mourning, and then there is a time to pick up the grief and continue living. This life of living with grief happens with peace when we no longer resist the very thing we are called to welcome. We know this, of course, because Christ himself declared that in this world we will have trouble. But let us not forget what was said just before and just after those words. "I have told you these things, so that in me you may have peace. In this world you will have trouble. But take heart! I have overcome the world" (John 16:33 NIV).

In Jesus, we have peace, even amid the grief.

As Jayber Crow, Wendell Berry's pensive protagonist in his book of the same name, so astutely observed, "I don't believe that grief passes away. It has its time and place forever. More time is

---

[3]Michelle Zauner, *Crying in H Mart* (New York: Vintage Books, 2023), 6.

added to it; it becomes a story within a story. But grief and griever alike endure."[4]

I think grief is like an ever-changing rock. Often, it is the size of a pebble. But a pebble in the bottom of your shoe, if you attempt to ignore it or continue on your journey despite it being there, is hurtful. If instead we pick the pebble up and put it in our pocket or a bag on our shoulder, well, suddenly it's a lot easier to carry on with it. And on the days when the pebble turns into a stone, or even a boulder, we need to be equipped to carry it. If we have already situated it in a manner that allows us to carry it, then we can continue, even on the days when it is particularly heavy. This is life lived with grief. Endured.

If we are really lucky, we have others journeying with us who acknowledge our grief and help us as we carry it. This, too, is countercultural. If we are able to be the type of friends who remember the long-suffering of the grieving, we can help alleviate that burden just a bit. We can help each other be more seen and, therefore, loved as we endure. Demon Copperhead, the lead character in Barbara Kingsolver's book by the same name, took the words right out of my mouth when he described his experience of enduring the grief of his mother's death. Demon says, "It's more like this bag of gravel I'm hauling around every day of the year. If somebody else brings it up, honestly, I'm glad of it. Like just for that minute they help me drag the gravel."[5] More rocks. As I read those words, I thought, "Yep. That's it." The gift of someone seeing my grief, even this many years later, is so powerful.

---

[4]Wendell Berry, *Jayber Crow: The Life Story of Jayber Crow, Barber, of the Port William Membership, as Written by Himself* (Thorndike, ME: Thorndike Press, 2001), 147–48.

[5]Barbara Kingsolver, *Demon Copperhead* (New York: HarperCollins, 2022), 243.

Don't forget Jesus's words. This kind of life is full of beauty and peace. This is the paradox of grief. This is not the life I would have chosen. A life of so much grief. Welcoming it, welcoming the long-suffering nature of it, with peace and endurance, allows us to live life more fully.

Enduring is the job of the long-sufferer. It is a job we will all be assigned at some point in our lives. It is not what we would choose. But goodness can be found there when we allow patience and long-suffering to lead the way.

Was there grieving on Holy Saturday? The only answer I can come to is, of course there was. I imagine they were remembering Jesus as he stood outside Lazarus's tomb and also remembering his words of warning that this world would bring heartbreak. Goodness, I imagine they were wishing it was different, that grief was not part of the story. Yet there they were, in the middle of the greatest story to have ever happened, and here, in the middle of it all, was grief. The same will be true of our stories; grief will be there. If we can welcome it, offer patience, and step forward with a sense of the call to endure, we, too, will find the peace of God in the midst of it.

In his poem "The Loons Prove That Even before There Was a Word for Grief It Existed as Song," Jacques J. Rancourt writes,

> if only time were malleable if only
> we could hold our breath for as long
> as those loons that slip under our boat
> in summer & resurface a mile away
> into a place they did not choose[6]

[6] Jacques J. Rancourt, "The Loons Prove That Even before There Was a Word for Grief It Existed as Song," *Broken Spectre* (New Gloucester, ME:

Grief can feel that way sometimes. That if we could just dissolve ourselves or fast-forward until it was time to get to a new place, all would be well. But such is not the way of this world. Instead, we are called to live the life before us. And that life often requires us to welcome the long-suffering of grief.

The furnishings at the cabin are the same as they were in 1990. That was the year we expanded and remodeled the cabin and, as such, refurnished the new spaces. In the corner of the living room is a small tufted chair and ottoman. This is my mom's chair. It was the first chair she ever bought that was sized just for her. At five foot two, she would often sit on a chair or a couch and have her feet dangling above the floor like a child. But this chair fit her as if it was made just for her.

When she passed away, it was so tempting to leave the chair as a shrine, to not use it despite the fact that we always sat in the chair when she was alive. I can almost picture myself recoiling or bracing as someone would sit in her chair. And then I remembered a conversation I heard when Mom was working on furnishing the cabin all those years ago.

We were in a store picking out the new furniture for the cabin living room. This was in our hometown, since the furniture store options further north were so limited. I remember the salesman's eyes getting all sparkly when he heard about "our cabin up north," assuming we had a never-ending bank account funding the furniture purchase as he started showing us the more expensive options. My mom looked him straight in the eyes and said, "Regardless of the couches we buy, there will be kids in wet bathing suits sitting on them within moments of their delivery. This furniture is meant to be used. And I won't have anything in the cabin that limits life from being lived at the lake."

Alice James Books, 2021), https://poetry.lib.uidaho.edu/poems/the-loons-prove-that-even-before-there-was-a-word-for-grief-it-existed-as-song/.

That's it, isn't it. Life is meant to be lived. And living the life before us requires us to make room to carry grief as we endure.

The life before me was one without my mom. Holding the chair as a shrine would not hold that reality at bay. But it would prevent life from continuing on. I think of my daughter curled up in that chair and how she gets to experience a connection with the grandma she has never met. I think of the delight I feel when one of my friends sits in the chair and is surprised that it fits them, when usually their feet are left dangling above the floor just like my mom's. These little glimpses of life lived well and with joy, can, and I would say are designed to, exist alongside the enduring grief I carry. Life is for the living, and we must live the life before us.

CHAPTER ELEVEN

STAY IN PRAYER

"On earth as it is in heaven." —Matthew 6:10

I pray as I paddle. Often, it is just a whisper, just a single word.

"Lord."

"Jesus."

"Please."

At times I wonder if these even "count" as prayers. How can a single word be anything other than a desperate cry? Yet what I know about Jesus's essentials of prayer, given in the Lord's Prayer, is that, yes, there are petitions found in even those single words. There is reverence, a plea for forgiveness, a reminder of sustenance provided and to be counted on. And when I whisper out over the water, I join with generations past in praying the same.

Out on the water, it is quiet. It's late autumn and the tourists have all left the lake. It is just me as I sigh one of those one-word prayers. I look down at my paddle as I dip into the water once again, and I see ripples coming at me across the lake. There is a breeze that seems to have stirred from a nonexistent wind. It sends more ripples all around my paddleboard, and as I look up, I see the leaves of the trees around the lake. They are rustling. Or, actually, they are clapping.

> You will indeed go out with joy
> and be peacefully guided;
> the mountains and the hills will break into singing
> before you,
> and all the trees of the field will clap their hands.
> (Isa. 55:12)

Creation itself responds as we worship the Creator.

It is easy to marvel at creation. Watching a gorgeous sunset over the lake, the view from the mountaintop, the towering pines, or the smallest creatures all create a sense of awe. But if we are not careful, we worship the creation and not the Creator. As we marvel at the beauty of creation, those mountains and trees, the sunrise and sunset, we must marvel at the one who created it all. His very creation does the same. The mountains singing, the trees clapping.

Praying is communal. When we pray, we pray with Jesus and the generations. We also pray with the mountains and hills, the trees and the rocks. If I listen closely enough, I can hear Paradox herself uttering her words of praise.

The Psalms are an easily misunderstood book in the Bible. The first time I really paid attention to studying the book of Psalms, I set out to read it straight through. This was a mistake. They can feel repetitive, dare I say, gripey, and sometimes reading straight through that book felt like drudgery. I knew something was off, so I began to research the Psalms. As I learned more about this collection of prayers, I started to understand how they were read long ago, and how we are to read them today. The Psalter is meant to be dipped into every single day.

In the psalms, we find every human emotion displayed before God. As such, the psalms are designed to infiltrate all aspects of our prayer life. They are the prayer book of the Bible, as relevant for us today as they were thousands of years ago.

When I began the arduous process of becoming better acquainted with Holy Saturday, I had no idea how much the psalms were woven into the day. Yet they are, as you have seen in these pages, everywhere.

The psalms were surely on the lips of those there that Holy Saturday. We can say this with confidence because psalms are daily prayers. The Talmud offers a specific psalm to be prayed on each day. Saturday's psalm is Psalm 92. A prayer for Sabbath, a psalm of praise. It was also traditional to recite psalms when someone had passed away. This involved reciting psalms from the day they died throughout the seven-day mourning period known as shiva.[1] Psalms were being prayed that day.

What if we considered joining in this ancient tradition of praying the Psalms? Rather than consider it rote or routine, we could also begin to pray from the prayer book. That sounds lovely, but how do we do it? The Psalms can feel distant from our modern language. They can feel more like someone else's prayers than our own as we get lost in the words. Praying the Psalter seems wonderful, a way to join in with the generations, but without a guide or road map through them, it is easy to get lost.

We, however, do have a road map for the Psalms.

---

[1] Rabbi Or N. Rose, "The Book of Psalms," My Jewish Learning, accessed January 23, 2023, https://www.myjewishlearning.com/article/the-book-of-psalms/.

When the disciples requested of Jesus, "Teach us to pray" (Luke 11:1), he answered them with the Lord's Prayer. In so doing, Jesus was not eliminating the Psalter. Not at all. Instead, he was offering the answer to "How do we pray the Psalter?" with authenticity and earnestness.

During the Sermon on the Mount, Jesus first instructed on how not to pray, to not be like the hypocrites and the pagans. Jesus warned us to avoid showing off and grandstanding. Then he shared what we now call the Lord's Prayer,

> This, then, is how you should pray:
> "Our Father in heaven,
> hallowed be your name,
> your kingdom come,
> your will be done,
> on earth as it is in heaven.
> Give us today our daily bread.
> And forgive us our debts,
> as we also have forgiven our debtors.
> And lead us not into temptation,
> but deliver us from the evil one." (Matt. 6:9–13 NIV)

The Psalms are what we are to pray. The Lord's Prayer is how we are to pray them. Each line of the Lord's Prayer is a type of statement or petition. Within the entire Psalter, we see psalms that reflect these petitions. When asked how to pray, Jesus's answer is to focus here, on these petitions. As we look at the Psalter, using this road map as our guide, we can find handles to grab on to as we begin to pray these prayers shared by generations upon generations.

In *Life Together*, Bonhoeffer mentions, almost as an aside, a profound truth: the idea that the whole Psalter is arranged according to the petitions of the Lord's Prayer.[2] What he meant was that Jesus drew the words of the Lord's Prayer out of the language of the Psalter. I believe we can better understand the Psalms if we look closely at the Lord's Prayer and its petitions. To know the Lord's Prayer is to know the heart of the Psalms.

It was a revelation to me when I first encountered this idea. The Lord's Prayer was something I memorized as a kid to make my father happy. I could spit it out in about six seconds, rapid-fire style. The Lord's Prayer was not something I spent much time pondering. But when we combine the notion that the Psalter was Jesus's prayer book and that the answer to "How do we pray?" is this profound prayer offered by Jesus, suddenly the whole thing becomes critical to comprehend.

There are seven petitions, that is, appeals or requests, found within the Lord's Prayer. Some of these petitions may be familiar, others less so. Let's walk through them briefly, though I encourage you to spend time dwelling on them. Each offers much insight and revelation, especially when approaching the Psalms. Once familiar with the petitions, you can read through the Psalms and see the petitions throughout. In my own Bible, I have taken to writing the petition number next to verses as I work my way through the psalms. Putting these two things together gives new insight into both the Lord's Prayer and the Psalter. Let's walk through the petitions one by one.

PETITION ONE: HOLY

Our Father in heaven, hallowed be your name

---

[2] Bonhoeffer mentions that he first saw this idea in Friedrich Oetinger's exegesis of the Psalms. See Dietrich Bonhoeffer, *Life Together and Prayerbook of the Bible*, Dietrich Bonhoeffer Works, vol. 5 (Minneapolis: Fortress Press, 1996), 58.

The Lord is holy. He is revered (hallowed), and we honor his holiness. This is a reminder to hold a place of reverence for the Lord, to remember his place and, therefore, ours as well. When we recall God's holiness with reverence, we are acknowledging his righteousness and the amazing gift it is that we get to approach him without fear. We acknowledge that he is worthy of worship. Psalm 8:1 declares, "LORD, our Lord, how magnificent is your name throughout the earth!" When we pray, we, too, declare him to be magnificent.

PETITION TWO: KINGDOM

Your kingdom come

The order of heaven is good and right, and may it be present here and now. Jesus said the kingdom of God was at hand, and therefore, we must consider how we can partner with God to be a place of welcome to the kingdom. This is a call for us to demonstrate the goodness of God and ask him to help us be a conduit of that goodness today, and a call of action for God to continue to restore and make all things new. When we pray, we plead for the righting of all wrongs and ask God how we can be partners in that good work.

PETITION THREE: SOVEREIGN

Your will be done, on earth as it is in heaven

God is sovereign. May his autonomy and sovereignty reign and bring perfection here, as they continue to do in heaven. Psalm 47:8 says, "God reigns over the nations." Acknowledging his reign and sovereignty is a means of affirming how good it is to be his people. When we pray with gratitude for his sovereignty, remembering it is rooted in love, we recognize the joy it is to be in the Father's will.

PETITION FOUR: PROVISION

Give us this day our daily bread

We seek and recognize provision for the immediate. It is not a call for excess or excessive blessing but instead a call to stay tethered to God and our need for his provision. Here we acknowledge our total reliance on Jesus for all that we have and need and welcome his daily provision so that we stay firmly tethered. Daily Jesus. Daily manna. When we pray with this petition, we are asking for what we need to get through the moment. We pray for provision recognizing that all good gifts come from God, that he will give us all we need.

PETITION FIVE: FORGIVE

And forgive us our debts (offenses) as we forgive those that have offended us

Help us to have forgiveness like Jesus. And help us recognize our own sin and need for forgiveness. This is a call for us to offer radical forgiveness, just as we have experienced radical forgiveness. We pray with a gratitude that acknowledges the forgiveness we have been given. We pray to be equipped to offer the same kind of forgiveness to those who have sinned against us. We pray to live like Jesus.

PETITION SIX: DIRECT

Lead us not into temptation

Do not let us yield to temptation. We recognize that we have the decision to make within our free will, and therefore, we ask God's help. This is a recognition of our propensity to turn away and a prayer against it. When we pray, we ask for God to direct our path and for our faith to hold fast. We pray with the psalmist, "Your word is a lamp for my feet and a light on my path" (Ps. 119:105). We pray for the Lord to lead us and for us to follow.

PETITION SEVEN: PROTECT

Deliver us from evil

Protect us from spiritual forces around us. This is not an expectation of shielding from evil but rather an acknowledgment of the existence of such powers in a fallen world and a plea for protection as we face them. We pray for courage and for clarity as we recognize there is an enemy fighting against us. Psalm 16:10 says, "For you will not abandon me to Sheol, you will not allow your faithful one to see decay." When we pray, we declare that God will not abandon us.

These petitions are found throughout the psalms. Sometimes you see one or two petitions within a single psalm, sometimes more. But taken as a whole, throughout the Psalter we see them all.

Sometimes on a Holy Saturday, or in a Holy Saturday season, prayer seems out of reach. Or maybe just the weight of everything makes it hard to pray. In moments like these, we can turn to the Lord's Prayer or to the Psalms and find the next word to say. Even better: we can find words to pray together. Just as they have offered guidance for thousands of years and for millions upon millions of believers, these words can be our strength when we don't know what to say.

Praying is not formulaic, it's communal. The beauty of understanding the psalms as part of a bigger story about prayer and believers coming together allows us to see them as vibrant, dynamic offerings that root us in truth, remind us of God's goodness, and call us together.

I have a dear group of friends who share the vocation of writer with me. We have formed a small cohort with the purpose of lifting each other up, encouraging each other in ways that are not just vocational but, among other things, spiritual. Last year we had our first weeklong retreat, and we had it at the cabin. The time was rich and deep and meaningful.

Our days were filled with conversation and quiet and fun and food. We took turns in the "hot seat" processing big things and had a daily roundtable check-in over the smaller things. But before any of that happened each day, we prayed together.

Every morning, we would come out of our rooms, head to the kitchen for coffee or tea and some toast, grab blankets to wrap around our shoulders, and then find our way to the porch. The "dreamy porch" as Sara called it. It is the favorite spot at the cabin for good reason. The porch has the best views of the lake, worn wood, and the original camp furniture from the 1950s. It wraps around the exterior of the original cabin structure like arms offering a constant hug. While sitting on the porch, you feel like you are simultaneously hovering in the forest and over the lake. Sara is right, it's dreamy. Paying no heed to the cool May air of upstate New York, we were determined to spend as much time on the porch as we could during our retreat.

Within the first twenty-four hours, we had each claimed our spot on the porch. Each morning, we would settle in to our respective spots, steaming mugs in our hands, and collectively exhale. We would gaze off at the trees or the water or the fog, lost in the nature for a few moments. Eventually, one of us would say, "Ready?" And then we would begin.

Sara had brought a liturgy of response and petition that we worked through every morning. On the first morning, I wasn't quite sure if using the same liturgy for all five days would be impactful. Surely, we would be simply reciting words by the end of day two or three, I imagined. Don't get me wrong, I love the *Book of Common Prayer* and have found a profound sense of unity in reciting Scripture as a congregation. But I was unsure as to how it would play out with just a handful of us coming back to the same few verses day after day. Would we encounter something divine?

I can assure you, we did. We took turns leading the liturgy, and then, in unison, we would say, *pray*, these first few verses of the first Psalm.

> Blessed is the one
>   who does not walk in step with the wicked
> or stand in the way that sinners take
>   or sit in the company of mockers,
> but whose delight is in the law of the LORD,
>   and who meditates on his law day and night.
> That person is like a tree planted by streams of water,
>   which yields its fruit in season
> and whose leaf does not wither—
>   whatever they do prospers. (Ps. 1:1–3 NIV)

Our voices carried out through the screens and onto the water as we prayed together. We could hear the birds chirping, the waves lapping, creation joining with us as we worshiped and prayed. Each morning different words jumped out. There, I was yearning for streams of water. The next day, I was praying with the psalmist that my leaves would not wither. The following day praying for my friend and the fruit to come after a season of toiling.

By the last morning, the words were pouring out of us, not from memorization but because they had been woven into our souls and each other. We were unified, together. Each word prayed on our own behalf and for the others among us. As we joined together, as the words drifted into the Adirondack spring air, it was a blessing and a prayer for us and for all who could hear. The lake was nearly empty in early May, yet we joined with creation and prayed.

PART FOUR

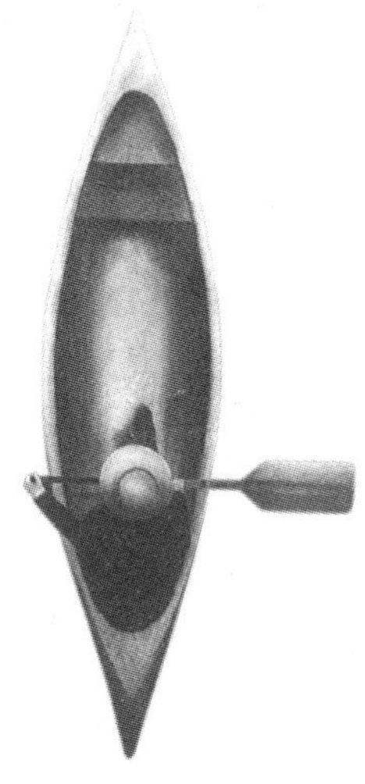

CHAPTER TWELVE

DESCEND AND ASCEND

"Therefore we were buried with him by baptism into death, in order that, just as Christ was raised from the dead by the glory of the Father, so we too may walk in newness of life." —Romans 6:4

The only way to get to the lake is to come down a super steep hill. *Super* steep. I take for granted how shocking it is for someone to see the hill for the first time. After a long straight stretch off the main road, the drive turns to the left, and you see the lake straight ahead, but the road seemingly gives out from under you. The hill before you is so steep you cannot see the road under your car any longer. To your right, nailed onto a tree, is a sign that reads, "Cardiac Hill. Dead Slow." A heart-stopping descent.

I have traversed Cardiac Hill thousands of times. I have of course driven, and before that, been driven, up and down the hill. I have walked and run up and down that hill. For the first eight years of life at the cabin, the communal washing machines were at the top of Cardiac Hill, so I would often walk alongside my mom as we lugged laundry baskets up and down the impossible incline. Much to my mother's chagrin, I have even ridden Big Wheels down the hill, at breakneck speed, I might add. If you aren't familiar with Big Wheels, they are low-seated tricycles with hard plastic wheels that offer zero traction, and for good measure, the contraption lacks any means of braking. We would watch for moments when the moms were thoroughly engaged in conversation on the child-free beach and would drag the Big Wheels up to the top of the hill. Once at the crest of Cardiac Hill, we would sit on our Big Wheels and lean forward just a fraction, and gravity did the rest. We were flying at heart-racing speeds, our legs sticking straight out, unable to pedal as fast as we were moving, laughing at the notion of "dead slow."

These days my kids are the ones running down Cardiac. And I can only imagine how my mom felt as she heard the crunching of gravel under those hard plastic tires as we came careening down the hill. As my kids' steps become faster and faster, I want to tell them to slow down. I begin to picture everything that could go wrong as they crash into the ground, the descent steeper than they imagine. Yet there they are, hair flying behind them, arms stretched out. They don't resist the descent; they welcome it with joy.

When asking friends to reflect on their time at the lake, more than one starts out by saying, "And that hill!" It is daunting. I have received phone calls and texts from friends at the top of Cardiac Hill asking if they are in the right place and wondering if perhaps there is another way to get to the lake.

"You are headed in the right direction," I reply. "The only way to get there is to head straight down."

Our ascent is only possible after a descent. One requires the other. We must remember this as we sit at the bottom of a pit or find ourselves careening down a never-ending hill. To have an ascent, we must first experience a descent.

This is key to understanding Jesus's life and the lives we are called to live in response. His mission was one of descents. Jesus descended at the incarnation; he descended when baptized; he descended at death. Down, down, down he went. God made himself ever more lowly so that we could live a life of ascents.

The first descent was the incarnation. Incarnation is the amazing gift of grace that Christ, the Son of God, became human—flesh, blood, bones. We call this the hypostatic union, which is a fancy way of saying he was fully human while remaining fully God. John 1:14 tells us, "The Word became flesh and dwelt among us. We observed his glory, the glory as the one and only Son from the Father, full of grace and truth."

The Word, from the Greek word *logos*, is Jesus. "Became flesh" refers to his act of fully taking on human nature. The incarnation. This is a descent. And he dwelt, or more rightly translated, he tabernacled among us. The tabernacle was the temporary, portable dwelling place of God in the Old Testament. Now, we find God himself, as a human, dwelling among us. God left the heights of heaven and lowered himself not just to *be* among us but to dwell and *live* among us. He shared his presence with us. The Lord became low.

The second descent was the baptism of Jesus. Jesus was baptized, but not as an act of repentance. A life lived without sin, as only Jesus's life was, does not warrant repentance. No, this baptism was something else.

In descending into the waters, Jesus symbolically demonstrated that he was giving up his will to the Father. The baptism, therefore, became a symbol for us all. Descending into the water and into the Father's will.

And here is the coolest part, this act of descent was met with the unity of the Trinity. Jesus descended into the water. As he came up out of the water, the Holy Spirit descended onto him, bringing the light with him. This was followed by the voice of the Father descending to earth, claiming Jesus as his Son and proclaiming his pleasure in Jesus's descent. Father, Spirit, Son.

And from this low place, Jesus's earthly ministry began, empowered by the Holy Spirit, blessed by God the Father. A ministry marked by Jesus's willingness to lower himself again and again and again and again.

Which brings us to the final descent of death. Being fully man, Jesus experienced a fully human death. This was the defining descent. The body of Jesus dead and buried in the tomb. This was the turning point of his ministry and for all of human history. The ultimate turnaround happens from this point. The descent of death giving way to resurrected life.

In *He Descended to the Dead*, Matthew Emerson describes this moment as the fulcrum between the descents and the ascents of Christ:

> From that low point, the rest of Christ's work—namely, his resurrection and ascension—is an ascent back to his Father. The descent stands as the fulcrum between these two movements. It is both the result of his death on the cross, in that he experiences not only the moment but also the state of death. But, as we have repeatedly seen, it is also and primarily understood as the beginning of Christ's exaltation.[1]

---

[1] Matthew Y. Emerson, *"He Descended to the Dead": An Evangelical Theology of Holy Saturday* (Downers Grove, IL: InterVarsity Press, 2019), 191.

The final descent, the death of Jesus, is a paradox. Both the end and the beginning.

Reading through Emerson's book, a single phrase jumped off the page to me, "an ascent back to his Father." Isn't that what we live as we walk out the Christian faith? We work our way back to God. And as we do, we rise.

The descents pave the way for the ascents. And it is this final descent into death that is the pivot point for the ascents to follow.

If Jesus came to us in descents, perhaps it was to make the way for a series of ascents that we are called to live. We live the descents in reverse, if you will. We experience rebirth in him, go on to live in freedom, and finally, enjoy life eternal. The descents become ascents.

Death begets life. This is the great paradox of Holy Saturday.

Christ's death becomes our fulcrum point as well. When we participate in that death, we, too, experience a turning upside down of our own world. We first welcome the death of self and all the good deaths Jesus calls us to.[2] As followers of Jesus, we then demonstrate new life through baptism. And from there, we live a life of freedom, pursuing Christ all the way to eternity. We rise and we rise and we rise.

In all of this waiting and long-suffering, in the praying and lamenting and keeping watch, may we remember that this is living the life Christ has before us. This is our rising. The apostle Paul wrote about the power of the resurrection in Ephesians, and he quoted Psalm 68:18.

> This is why it says:
> "When he ascended on high,

---

[2] For more on the death of self, see Jessica Herberger, *Life Surrendered: Finding Freedom at the Cross* (Abilene, TX: Leafwood, 2022).

> he took many captives
> and gave gifts to his people." (Eph. 4:8 NIV)

Notice Paul explains that the phrase "he ascended" implied that "he also descended to the lower, earthly regions? He [Jesus] who descended is the very one who ascended higher than all the heavens, in order to fill the whole universe" (Eph. 4:9–10 NIV). Our rising can only be understood in light of Christ's descent. We celebrate Christ's ascension, as we should, but so often we neglect to consider the descents that came first. In Christ's rising, he takes us captive. We are swept up into the redeemed humanity forged in the descents of Jesus.

Our ascent, our journey back to the Father, happens because of the descents. Jesus died so we may live. As we remember this, we have communion with him in our descents, which bring our rising.

This is the overarching view of ascents and descents for the life of a believer. But on a much smaller scale, the moment to moment life we live, we experience ascents *and* descents over and over. As we go through life, we are faced with trials and disappointments, trauma and disaster, and each of these descents are part of the journey. Understanding the notion of a fulcrum helps us see how God is working in and through us to draw us closer to him. So we can continue ever rising closer, experiencing greater intimacy with God.

The ascents are beautiful. The glimpses of ease when all is so evidently well and good that we can exhale and catch our breath. For some of us, they are far too scarce. Yet they do exist. These are the literal ups and downs of life. Each one presents a fulcrum opportunity, a moment of turnaround, when we begin to ascend again.

Seeing the big picture helps us stay steady in the small picture. Seeing the rising, rising, rising we are invited to as we continue to practice faithfulness and grow closer to God helps us hold our peace as we descend again.

The Adirondack Mountains, Adirondack Park's namesake, are an impressive, sweeping collection of 1,606 mountains. Among the massive group of mountains is a group of the "high peaks." This collection of the forty-six highest mountains, all over 4,000 feet high, stand above the rest.[3] The Adirondacks were named in 1838 by Professor Emmons, a local geologist, to commemorate the Native Americans who called them home.[4] About fifty-five years later, the mountains and the surrounding land were deemed a Forever Wild Forest Preserve (one of the first in the country) and a National Historic Landmark known as the Adirondack Park.

The first documented climb of one of the high peaks occurred by 1918, and on June 10, 1925, Herbert Clark (considered "46er" #1) and George (#2) and Robert Marshall (#3) climbed their forty-sixth high peak, Mt. Emmons. This is where things got interesting. The idea of climbing this impressive group of peaks caught the attention of Edward Hudowalski of Troy, New York (a few hours away from the high peaks). He led his Sunday school class on a backpacking trip to climb Marcy, Basin, and Saddleback. From there, the pastor of Edward's church caught the hiking bug, and together, the two men formed a hiking club called the Forty-Sixers.[5] This hiking club still exists today, some seventy-five years later. To be a

[3] Four of the forty-six have recently been measured to be less than 4,000 feet yet retain the title of high peak.

[4] Alfred L Donaldson, *A History of the Adirondacks* (Harrison, NY: Harbor Hill Books, 1977), 36.

[5] "Timeline," Adirondack 46ers, accessed May 29, 2023, https://adk46er.org/timeline/.

"46er" designates that one has hiked all forty-six high peaks and is a true badge of honor.

Edward's wife, Grace (#9 and the first female 46er), became the club's historian and a champion of the peaks. Grace was known to sing hymns as a means of encouragement to the tired hikers as they climbed up, up, up.

> Hark! I hear Hope sweetly singing
> Softly in an undertone,
> Singing as if God had taught her,
> "It is better farther on."

Such hymn singing began the practice of vespers on the mountain. Recognizing that most of their hikers had only one free day during the week, Sunday, and that they would not want to forsake worship, the Forty-Sixers began holding evening worship services after the climb. Singing hymns, reading psalms, and listening to a message all became part of the celebration at the summit. Nearly every Forty-Sixers vespers message is focused on the same thing, "It's not only about getting to the top, but about the knowledge, satisfaction, and inspiration gained from the climbing experience."[6]

Having climbed a high peak, both literally and figuratively, I can tell you that the view from the top is beautiful, but all the learning and formation happens on the way up and on the way down. I've stood atop Whiteface Mountain and been breathless at the beauty, worshiping the Creator. The summit is good. But it is not where we stay. Instead, we are most often ascending or descending, being pushed through, holding on for dear life, believing God is just as present at the bottom of the mountain as he is at the top.

---

[6] "Barb Traver Vespers Message," Adirondack 46ers, accessed May 29, 2023, https://adk46er.org/barb-traver-vespers-message/.

That is the thing about mountains. There are always more to climb. And the only way to go from one summit to another is to descend. The next ascent awaits, but first we must, once again, welcome the descent.

CHAPTER THIRTEEN

THE LIGHT

"Then God said, 'Let there be light,' and there was light."
—Genesis 1:3

Golden hour at the lake is all you could ever hope it to be. Our sweeping screen porch faces not just the lake and the mountains but also the sunset. We marvel at the beauty as the sky is painted shades of pink and orange and gold. The porch is bathed in gold. It touches every surface and will steal your breath away every single time you see it.

It is the most beautiful light I have ever seen.

It is as if all of creation is celebrating that God said, "Yes, let there be light again today." And as the day comes to a close, there is one last beautiful moment of light for us to hold on to. The glow of the sky and the reflections on the water, the way the kids still swimming turn to silhouettes against it, all is divine.

The light touches everything. It goes everywhere. How grateful I am that it is so.

In Jewish tradition, it is in those moments of golden hour, as the sun is preparing to set, that the Sabbath candles are lit. The lights are aflame, ready to welcome the dark, to push it back. Rabbi Heschel explains, "Just as creation began with the word 'Let there be light!' so does the celebration of creation [the Sabbath] begin with the kindling of lights."[1] The imagery of light must have been particularly strong that Sabbath night as Jesus's body lay in the cold tomb. The juxtaposition of light and dark perhaps never greater. How perfectly fitting that this day of darkness, this day of waiting and in-between, was also ordained to be the Sabbath, a day of light.

Lighting the Sabbath candles that night, Holy Saturday, must have been profound. To light the candles and recite, "Blessed are you, Lord our God, King of the universe, who has made us holy through his commandments and commanded us to kindle the Sabbath light." Just as the darkness was set to close in, the Sabbath candles bring forth light.

How deeply the light was needed that night as they all fought the darkness. To be in a place of darkness and yet be commanded to bring the light. This is the work of Sabbath, the work that carries on. The light is needed because the darkness is so heavy. King David describes the weight of darkness beautifully:

> The ropes of death were wrapped around me;
> the torrents of destruction terrified me.
> The ropes of Sheol entangled me;
> the snares of death confronted me.
> I called to the Lord in my distress,
> and I cried to my God for help.

[1]Abraham Joshua Heschel, *The Sabbath: Its Meaning for Modern Man* (New York: Farrar, Straus and Giroux, 2005), 66.

> From his temple he heard my voice,
> and my cry to him reached his ears. (Ps. 18:4–6)

Death, destruction, Sheol. This is the darkness. And David's cry reached God's ears. As the psalm draws to a close, we see the answer God gave as David points us back to the light and, even more importantly, the source of the light.

> Lord, you light my lamp;
> my God illuminates my darkness. (Ps. 18:28)

God illuminates the darkness. When we are facing the darkness of the unknown, we must remember God himself illuminates even the darkness. He is the one who lights the darkness.

When I was younger, before the expansive porch was added, and the tiffany lamp with it, we would have to use a camping gas lantern for light on the porch. To me, it was a magical thing. My mom would turn on the propane, light the lantern, and somehow the mesh mantel would hold the light and never catch on fire. I can still hear the sound of the gas whirring as what was dark became light. It was the power of the light that was most amazing to me.

Creating daylight when there was night. Light in the darkness. This is what God does for us. With him, through him, all the darkness fades.

In Psalms, David speaks of his lamp, lit by God. Consider, too, what Proverbs says about the connection between our spirit and the lamp. "The human spirit is the lamp of the Lord that sheds light on one's inmost being" (20:27 NIV). For us to know ourselves, we must use the lamp of God to look at ourselves. This knowing comes from God, and our very spirit, when entrusted to Christ, becomes the lamp of God equipped to do that good work.

Exploring the connection between light and the soul in Jewish thought, Rabbi Yehuda Shurpin summarizes a medieval rabbi's commentary on the topic. "Rabbi Bechayei ben Asher (1255–1340) explains that the soul derives joy from the candle's light. . . . The soul is made up of divine light, and it is natural to delight in something that is of a similar makeup. This is the case even though the candle generates mere physical light, whereas the soul's light is spiritual."[2] This may sound a bit strange to our modern sensibilities. But I think Rabbi Bechayei is on to something. We are drawn to light because we recognize it as a symbol of God. Innately, we know that God brings the light and is responsible for the light within us.

Just about the time that David wrote Psalm 18, he also was writing 2 Samuel.[3] David, near the end of his life, was looking back at all that had happened. He defeated Goliath; he survived the many years of hiding from Saul; he became king and brought much honor to the people of God through victories on the battlefield; he established Jerusalem and reclaimed the ark of the covenant. His life was full of so many accomplishments and adversaries. As he reflected on his victory and the power that got him through the darkness of battle, he wrote:

> LORD, you are my lamp;
> The LORD illuminates my darkness.
> With you I can attack a barricade,
> and with my God I can leap over a wall.
> (2 Sam. 22:29–30)

God was the lamp he carried with him and the source of illumination. The light went with David as he faced the darkness. The light

---

[2] Yehuda Shurpin, "Why Do We Light a Yahrtzeit Memorial Candle?" Chabad.org, accessed March 6, 2023, https://www.chabad.org/library/article_cdo/aid/3034297/jewish/Why-Do-We-Light-a-Yahrtzeit-Memorial-Candle.htm#footnote6a3034297.

[3] "Probable Timeline of When Each Psalm Was Written - Study Resources," Blue Letter Bible, accessed March 5, 2023, https://www.blueletterbible.org/study/parallel/paral18.cfm.

went with him just as it goes with us today. The light, the same one that Proverbs 20:27 speaks to, comes through Jesus.

We know, almost intrinsically, that "in the beginning was the Word" (John 1:1), but do we consider the verses that follow? The Gospel of John goes on to say that in Jesus was life and "that life was the light of men" (John 1:4). The very light we need comes directly from within Jesus. "I am the light of the world. Anyone who follows me will never walk in the darkness but will have the light of life," Jesus said in John 8:12. To follow Jesus is to have the light of life with you at all times. It is your lamp; it is in your soul. As such, you are never without it. The light goes with you. The light is with you in every dark moment, every long night, every second of wondering, every instance of worrying. These are not empty platitudes. This is a promise from Jesus himself, "I have come as light into the world, so that everyone who believes in me would not remain in darkness" (John 12:46). Why did Jesus come as the light of the world? He came for you and for me, so we would not be overcome by the darkness because we get to carry his light within us.

In *Hinds' Feet on High Places*, we follow a girl through an arduous journey up a mountain. Along the way, she learns powerful lessons about herself and her Creator. Finally, atop the summit, she understands the gift of the journey she has been on.

> Paradoxical as it may seem, as she gazed out on the dazzling vistas, so glorious that she could not look at them steadily or grasp their magnificent sweep, she often thought that the prayer which best expressed her heart's desire was that of the blind man. "Lord, that I might receive my sight! Help me to open myself to more light."[4]

[4]Hannah Hurnard, *Hinds' Feet on High Places: An Engaging Visual Journey* (Carol Stream, IL: Tyndale, 2017), 120.

It is really all about the light. And because of Jesus, we get to open ourselves to more and more light.

This is a powerful reminder for us as we face darkness. The light we carry with us, the light of Christ, is powerful enough for all that we may face. It is the light that broke through hell, it is the light that was with King David, and it is the light within us. I wonder if perhaps we don't marvel at that enough.

Holy Saturday is a dark day. Both the actual Holy Saturday of Holy Week and the Holy Saturdays we face. When the world seems dark, still the light comes through. I can think of nothing more hopeful to get me through the long nights of darkness. The light casts out fear and worry; the light brings goodness into hard places; it is the light of God himself. And dear reader, it is in you. The light goes with you wherever you go, whatever you face. This changes everything as we face Holy Saturdays, as we face grief, keep watch, and continue to trust. The light goes with us.

As a girl I would spend hours below the surface of the lake, exploring. The area in between our little beach and the big beach is a rocky section perfect for "diving expeditions." In between the rocks and pebbles, I would find innumerable treasures. Mussel shells, snail shells, crayfish, sparkling rocks. I would push off the rocks and dive down the few feet to the bottom, wait for the water to settle, and feel like I was in my own little underwater world. I felt invisible to the world outside of the water.

Now my kids are the ones swimming in the lake, and I am watching from my perch on our porch. I tell them my tales of diving for hours and the joy it brought me. They are unsure. What unknown things could the depths of the lake hold? Will the rocks be slimy? How could it look any different than it does from up above?

From above, the water looks dark, the bottom impossible to see. My daughter, deciding to be brave, puts on her goggles and dives down off "the big rock," exploring the bottom of the lake. I see nothing except the deep blue surface of the water.

With great excitement, she breaks through the surface and tells me of all the treasures she found below, fish and shells and pebbles and plants, and how the streams of light break through the water all the way to the bottom. She is amazed at the world below that she has discovered in the rays of sunshine that make their way to the bottom of the lake. I smile because she has figured it out. The light follows you down.

No matter how dark it may appear, the light breaks through.

How differently would I handle those dark nights if I were to remember the light I carry with me. As we consider what Holy Saturday has to teach us for our in-between moments, our days of desperation, and the time we spend waiting for resurrection, I wonder if this could be the most comforting thing to remember.

The light, our light, illuminated by God, is with us always, for our comfort and to show the world the light.

And in its glow, darkness flees.

BENEDICTION

The Paradox

When the sun is long done setting and the sky is dark, especially on a night when the clouds are blocking the moon and stars, we sit on the porch and watch for the lights across the lake. One by one we see little rectangles of light appear as the cabins across the way send out beacons glowing on the water. Paradox is not very populated, so most nights we can count the lights off pretty easily. Each block of light is a sign of life.

Staring out at the black night sky and the black waters can feel pretty melancholy without those lights of life on the opposite shore. And it occurs to me, we must be the same thing for them. Our light a sign of life for those watching.

I wonder if that is how it is when we remember the light we have within us. Could it be that our light reminds others of life being lived? I think it must be. We are drawn to the light, and we get to be the light.

As I type out these last words, I am still in my tiny writing office, looking out at the birds as they land on the branches of the mighty pines. It is finally spring, and the robins and sparrows are busy. The half-broken chair I had at the beginning of writing the book has collapsed and been replaced. Where before it faced only the black wall, my desk now sits at the corner where the black wall meets the white one. The walls meet and form a line running down, separating dark from light. New life wherever I look. That seems right as we close out our study of this day. We started in total darkness, and while we are not yet in the glory of resurrection, the light and the dark have met—total darkness is no longer the view.

Life continues on. The paradoxes are everywhere. There are ascents and descents that seem never-ending. As we have worked through all that happened on this day so long ago, and all that it means for us today, we, too, have cycled through ups and downs. When I began the process of writing this book, I drew a map of where we would go, each chapter pointing up or down. The arrows, even the ones pointing down, ascended across the page. Chapter by chapter, we have risen.

Living out Holy Saturday—whether in a tragic loss, an unexpected change, a crisis, a disappointment, or just the ins and outs of daily life—is a mix of ups and downs. But over time, the ups and downs will cause us to rise if we let them.

The descent that leads to ascent.

Dead yet alive.

Grieving yet comforted.

Lamenting yet hopeful.

Resting and keeping watch, remembering and praying, gathering. Holding on to the light. This is living the life before us, faithfully. Days filled with peace as we wait for the light to break all the way through.

Writing this book has been an exercise in perseverance and faithfulness. It has been a strange season of heaviness and darkness. Almost all of the book was written during the winter months when I was far away from Paradox. Even through the spring months that followed, things were off, so much so that I wasn't able to get a paddle into the water until the first week of July. As we settled into lake life for the week, I was itching to paddle. Rain and projects needing attention kept me away for the first few days. Finally, on the Fourth of July, I slipped my boat into the water and took off.

The need to go on this paddle was so deep within me. The previous few weeks in particular had been incredibly heavy, and I was feeling so disconnected from the goodness I know can be present amidst the dark—I was seeking peace and light. So I headed to Dead Boy's Island.

It was a perfect day with puffy white clouds in the brilliant blue sky. I wanted to get eyes on the island and fact check myself. One last book task before we could call this book done.

As soon as I put my paddle in the water, I could feel peace settle over me. As I made my way through Smith Bay, I prayed and sang and felt such communion with God. As I saw Dead Boy's Island, the rays of sunshine coming down on to the pine trees was breathtaking. Approaching the island, I decided against going ashore and instead opted to circumnavigate in my kayak. Coming around the far side of the island I noticed a patch of marshy grass and held my breath. *Could it be?* I wondered.

One paddle closer confirmed my hopeful wondering. There about eighteen inches away from the tip of my boat was the loon, sitting on her nest, protecting this year's eggs. New life just about to break through. I have never been able to find the loon nest on our lake. Year after year I have looked, and never once had I been successful. Until now, on Dead Boy's Island. Life found in the place of death.

Looking up I was greeted by a paddleboarder coming around the island from the other direction. I motioned to be quiet and pointed toward the loon. We both paddled in place, amazed at the discovery. The paddler must have sensed I knew a bit about the loon and started asking questions about them. The nature lesson moved on to neighborly banter as we sorted out where each other's our cabins were. When my new friend heard we were at Summer Haven she said, "Oh! I love your sign." Beaming, I replied, "My mom designed that," as I wiped a tear away. We chatted for a few more minutes and then both confessed we had to get going as Fourth of July festivities were awaiting our attention. I paddled through a swath of water lilies as I headed back into the bay that leads me home and exhaled more than I had in the last six months, overwhelmed with gratitude.

Life, I thought. *It's still here.*

As I made my way back to our beach, I realized this one paddle, the one that had caused me to exhale and to feel peace again, had almost all the practices we have been reflecting on here. Remembering, trusting, praying, gathering, acknowledging where we are, and others all led me to the place of peace in the dark once again.

My prayer and hope are that you experience the same.

May we welcome the paradox of it all.

DISCUSSION GUIDE

Use this discussion guide to further your personal study, or gather a group together and process *Peace in the Dark* together. The guide is broken up into four sessions. Pick and choose what meeting schedule works for you. You can break each session into two and meet more than four times or just work through a handful of questions at a single gathering. May you be encouraged and strengthened as you spend time with the paradoxes, the ascents and descents, and the practices that bring us peace.

PART ONE

CHAPTER ONE: ACKNOWLEDGE WHERE YOU ARE

CHAPTER TWO: REMEMBER

CHAPTER THREE: BURY WELL

CHAPTER FOUR: REST

- As you began the book, what were your thoughts about Holy Saturday? Had you considered it before, and if so, what did you think?

- In Chapter One, Jessica shares a story about feeling lost because she had not fully acknowledged where she was. Is that something you have experienced? How can fully acknowledging where you are when something has gone wrong help you as you continue on?

- Is there someone in your life or in Scripture that you see as having lived through hard seasons faithfully? What have you observed about them? How can that help you as you journey through a Holy Saturday season?

- Have you had personal experience with burial? What peace have you felt as you walked through the steps of burial? How could that apply to burying other things that have died, such as a dream you had or a relationship?

- Do you rest well? What are the things in life making it harder to step fully into rest? Do you think rest is a mandate?

PART TWO

CHAPTER FIVE: THE BEAUTY OF LAMENT

CHAPTER SIX: STAND IN THE GAP

CHAPTER SEVEN: STILL WE GATHER

- When we talk of lament, do you feel uncomfortable? Can you articulate why? How have you responded to the lament that bubbles up inside of you or others?

- What is the connection between peace and lament? Does this make lament seem more accessible to you?

- Have you spent time considering what Jesus was doing as his body lay in the tomb? What have you considered after reading through Chapter Six?

- How does what Jesus did affect us today? How can we more willingly head to hell on a rescue mission?

- Have you gathered with a group of people faithfully for a long time? How comfortable are you showing up authentically, even though flawed? How can we be a place of welcome for others?

PART THREE

CHAPTER EIGHT: KEEP WATCH

CHAPTER NINE: TRUST GOD IS WORKING

CHAPTER TEN: WELCOME LONG-SUFFERING

CHAPTER ELEVEN: STAY IN PRAYER

- What is the purpose of bearing witness to others' pain? How can we push through our own discomfort to keep watch?

- Have you had seasons when it seemed like God had stopped working for your good? How did you stay tethered to your faith?

- How do the heroes of faith in Hebrews 11 help us to see with God's eyes, not our own?

- How can we be people who welcome the weight of grief and live life fully with the grief? How can we help others do the same?

- What methods of prayer do you tend to gravitate toward? How could trying different means of prayer enable you to stay in prayer during the Holy Saturday moments?

PART FOUR

CHAPTER TWELVE: DESCEND AND ASCEND

CHAPTER THIRTEEN: THE LIGHT

BENEDICTION: THE PARADOX

- How does understanding the big narrative of Christ's descents and our ascents help you as you consider the Christian life?

- Does thinking of Holy Saturday as a fulcrum change how you consider those kinds of seasons?

- With all the unknown and the difficulties that come with a Holy Saturday season, how does the notion of light change things? If the light is in us, is there ever darkness?

- Of all the paradoxes of Holy Saturday, which stood out to you the most?

- What practices resonated the most with you? What practices seem the most challenging to incorporate into your life? Do you know why that is?